LifeWorks *with*
SHELLI PELLY
presents:

RULES
FOR WOMEN & GIRLS

An Empowering Must-Read for Women,
Moms, and Daughters!

22 Badass Rules for Women & Girls

Copyright © 2018 by Shelli Pelly

All rights reserved. No part of this publication may be reproduced, stored in or introduced into a retrieval system, or transmitted, in any form, or by any means electronic, mechanical, printing, recording or otherwise, without the prior permission of the author and/or publisher.

Photos by Remy Haynes

Edited by Kelly Fleming

Cover Design and Interior Typesetting by Melissa Williams Design

ISBN: 978-1790615667

Published by LifeWorks by Shelli Pelly

~~21~~ 22 BADASS RULES
FOR WOMEN & GIRLS

An Empowering Must-Read for Women,
Moms, and Daughters!

LifeWorks *with*
SHELLI PELLY

LET'S CONNECT!
Share your feedback:

Facebook / Twitter / Instagram:
@LifeWorksSP

Press and Media, Email:
ToxicPebbles@gmail.com

CONTENTS

22 BADASS RULES
15 Things That Badass Women Do Differently Than Everyone Else

Badass STANDARDS: GUYS, DATING and RELATIONSHIPS

- #1   *Teach men how to treat you: Set your standards and stick to them.*
- #2   *No one puts Baby in a corner! You aren't anyone's Plan B.*
- #3   *Never chase a guy. Ever. If he's interested, he'll come to you.*
- #4   *When a guy tells you by his actions, who he is—believe him. The first time.*
- #5   *(6) Universal Red Flags that translate to: GAME OVER.*
- #6   *Keep the values that make you feel strong—release all the others.*
- #7   *Expect CHIVALRY: It does matter . . . and NO it is not sexist.*
- #8   *WAIT until he asks for Exclusivity.*
- #9   *Ending relationships, pull-off the band-aid fast and hard. It's less painful.*
- #10   *Watch how a man talks about and treats his mom. It'll tell you how he feels about women, and it's indicative of how he will treat you.*

Badass LIFE FUNDAMENTALS
#11 *Your life is 10% what happens to you, 90% how you handle it.*
#12 *The fine art of not giving a f*ck.*
#13 *Life's BIGGEST mistakes are made when we ignore our intuition.*
#14 *Live the life that makes YOU happy.*
#15 *The 5 people you spend the most time with, either add to detract from your life course. Choose mindfully and wisely.*
#16 *Understand that you always have the power of choice. Always.*

One Badass CAREER
#17 *80% of getting the job, is just not being an idiot.*
#18 *(6) best career practices for building "Good Reputation Equity".*

Badass LIFE STRATEGIES
#19 *Identify your key strengths, then leverage them. Don't waste time trying to be Britney.*
#20 *Slow your roll—hold your anger for 24-hours.*
#21 *Understand the power of your Personal Image. Let it communicate who you are and where you want to go, at-a-glance.*
#22 *Know your END-GAME. It will naturally drive decisions and actions towards your goal.*

22 BADASS Rules Checklist

ABOUT THE AUTHOR

22 BADASS RULES

Badass. Ask 5 different people to describe a badass woman, and you're likely to get 5 different descriptions. The old school connotation of a badass, conjured up images of a chain-smoking, tattooed, crass-talking, in-your-face, motorcycle-riding biker lady, who could squish you like a flea with her pinky finger. Not that there's anything wrong with that. Gulp.

In this book, I'm talking about a *modern-day badass woman*, which has nothing to do with her external appearance. That's too one-dimensional.

A Modern-Day Badass Woman:

Is a state-of-mind. It is a way of thinking, behaving and moving through the world with unapologetic self-confidence, uncompromising self-worth, assertiveness, compassion, independence, comfort in her own skin and grace under fire.

Under that definition, why *wouldn't* you want to be a badass? If you have daughters or nieces, undoubtedly you've worked to instill these types of character traits and strengths in her.

Whether you call it *badass*, or another word of your choosing, the point is—*we all want to feel authentically strong and empowered*. We want our *daughters* and other young women in our lives to be strong, self-assured and uphold boundaries that reinforce her self-worth and intrinsic value as a woman. *That is what* **22 Badass Rules** *will do.*

True badass vs. fake badass

A *true badass* doesn't hit others over the head with her badass-ness. She doesn't need to. Her aura of strength, independence, self-assuredness and confidence is palpable, without saying a word.

A *fake badass*, feels the need to constantly remind people. She comes across as overbearing, aggressive vs. assertive, trying too hard.

I liken it to the difference between 2 types of cars: Flashy, neon yellow Ferrari vs. Sleek, black Mercedes.

> The *Fake Badass* is like a neon yellow Ferrari. It's loud, flashy, noisy and screams "Look at me! Look at me!" It revs its engine in passing, making extra sure everyone sees, hears and is impressed by it.

The *True Badass* is like a sleek, black Mercedes. It's subtle and understated, but you *know* it's strong and powerful beneath the hood. In passing, it wryly smiles at you with a knowing wink.

You were born with it

As women, we were *all born* with a badass inside of us. Whether or not you choose to unleash it, is entirely up to you. Chances are, it's active in some areas of your life, dormant or at least more challenged, in others.

For example, a woman who is a force to be reckoned with in her professional life, systematically dates men who do not treat her well. A badass in her professional life, but not in her love life. That is her challenge area.

Everyone has areas to strengthen and that is what this book will offer.

Although we all have badass in us, learning to cultivate and unleash it is a learned process. We learn through listening, watching and applying the experiences of others, our parent's guidance, and most commonly—trial and error . . . life lessons that we have to learn on our own.

It's like the difference between being told not to touch the pot, it'll burn, and actually touching the pot and having to feel the searing pain for yourself. You're much more likely to learn the lesson if you've felt the burn firsthand.

22 Badass Rules. Don't Live Life Without Them.

The Rules are here to serve every woman, at every age and every stage of life. Whether you are married, divorced, single, 15, 35 or 65+ there is something here for every woman.

If you have daughters, nieces and young women that you care about—the 22 Rules outlined in this book are *essential* for her to have as a reference, as she navigates life.

Why? Because these Rules are timeless principles instilling *confidence and strength*, regardless of who or what is going on around you. It doesn't matter. *A Badasses opinion of herself does not change, based on external forces.*

The Rules are all about setting clear boundaries and standards based in self-respect, self-worth, confidence and independence, as they relate to everything from:

— Guys, dating and relationships.
— 6 Red Flags in a guy, that scream run don't walk.
— Why you always have the power of choice.
— The 10/90 Rule. Life is 10% what happens, 90% how you handle it.
— Follow your own life path, despite other's expectations.
— 6 Best Practices for long-term career success.
— Leverage your key strengths.
— Define your end-game first. It'll guide your actions to goal.
— Strength and confidence in the face of negative people and comments.

— Decisively walk away from people and situations that don't work for you.

For your daughters

Did you know that on average, we need to hear something *at least 3x* before it registers in our mind? That's why big companies like Coke and McDonald's will buy so many advertising slots in any 1 given program. They know it takes a few times before consumers "note" the ad.

It's also more effective to hear the message in different ways, from different sources. Think of this book as a secondary source for your daughters or other young women in your life.

My mom used to joke that my sister and I would listen to her more carefully if she didn't have "M.O.M" in front of her name. In truth, I *did* listen to her. I just didn't want her to know at the time. Yes, I was a handful. No, nothing's changed. The principles in this book are many of her teachings, that frankly were the guiding force behind our strength of self.

Keepin' It Real sections

Throughout the book, you'll see *Keepin' It Real* sections, where I share my own personal life experiences for a given topic. These are areas where I learned the hard way, fell flat on my face, figured it out, then got back up to try 'er again.

I'm not a fan of those who pontificate from an Ivory Tower (theoretical talk, little real-life experience). It rings hollow and candidly, it's kind of annoying. Chances are, if I'm writing about it, I've lived it, learned it and now I share it!

Before we dive into the 22 Rules—*let's see what badass women do differently* than everyone else! You have to know where you're going, if you want to get there—right?

15 Things That Badass Women Do Differently Than Everyone Else:

1. She is authentically self-confident

Her confidence is authentic, because she recognizes her own inherent value and what she brings to the table. She knows what works for her and what does not. Her confidence does not change, based on who likes her and who does not.

2. She is assertive, not aggressive

There's a difference. The *true badass* is assertive. She confidently states what she wants, presents her position firmly but calmly, standing her *ground*. A *fake badass* is aggressive, resorts to yelling, badgering and/or intimidating until someone makes something happen. *Assertive* women take charge and get things done themselves or through directive leadership.

3. She has clear boundaries.

She knows what she'll tolerate and what she won't. You may get off with a warning the first time you cross a boundary (she is fair, after-all) but she'll cut bait if you do it again.

4. She is her own best friend.

She is perfectly comfortable being alone, instead of settling for someone who drags her down, or tries to drag her off of her chosen path.

5. She won't quit, but she'll cut-bait if something isn't working for her.

She doesn't run away from a challenge, but she quickly grasps when it's a losing battle and will walk away. This saves her time, hassle and frees up time to work on things that *are* working in her life.

6. She doesn't waste her time on negative people.

She won't pretend that she likes you just for show, or to be part of a group. She will be coolly cordial if you run into her, but other than that she won't have any contact with you. If you've done something to her personally, she'll call you on it.

She learned this life lesson the hard way. She knows that some people and things are just not that worthy, and she lets them go.

7. Save the drama for your mama

She finds drama and mindless gossip a stupid, annoying waste of time. She has no interest in lowering herself to that level or dragging others through the mud just to make herself look better. She is a problem *solver*, not a problem *creator*.

8. She pursues the life *she* wants to live, not the one *other's* want her to live

She knows that she is the creator of her own life, her own destiny. She takes sole responsibility for her happiness, which is why she won't cave into anyone else's pressure to change course.

If she does inadvertently find herself on the wrong path, she has the courage to right the ship, make a plan and change course, whether she's 25, 45 or 65+.

9. She doesn't have FOMO (Fear of Missing Out)

A modern, badass woman doesn't care what everyone else is doing. She doesn't spend time worrying about celebrities, followers and "likes." She's focused on her own initiatives and doing things that *she* authentically wants to do.

10. She can't stand phony, fake people

A badass woman is confident. She doesn't feel the need to pretend that her life and relationships are *always* Instagram perfect, like a Stepford Wife.

Phoniness in others is her kryptonite. She smells shallow fakeness a mile away, and steers clear.

11. She doesn't chase guys

She is comfortable in her own skin, knows her value and is confident in what she brings to the table. Any guy worth his salt has to have the confidence to approach her. If he's too shy, he's not the guy for her. She will steamroll over him without meaning to. Women who are a catch, (you!) don't have to chase.

12. She learns from past mistakes

A badass woman gets to be badass, because she analyzes past mistakes, finds the lesson, and applies it to her life moving forward. She acknowledges mistakes and learns to do better. Other than that, she doesn't dwell on it and she certainly doesn't play the victim.

13. She lives by the 10/90 Rule

She understands that life is *10% what happens to you, 90% how you react to it.* A badass doesn't blame others for her situation, wallow in self-pity or waste time feeling sorry for herself. She looks at the hand she's dealt, then figures out a way to get to the cheese.

14. She isn't a victim. She's a fighter. She is resilient.

She knows that life throws curve balls and some are worse than others. She might allow herself a temporary pity party, but she's a fighter and she is resilient. Life might knock her down, but she'll put together a plan of action and like a Phoenix, get right back up, stronger and savvier than before.

15. She takes pride in, and care of herself

She knows that you can't drive a car on an empty tank. She makes herself first priority, nourishing herself with healthy foods, exercising, limiting alcohol, steering clear of drugs or smoking, taking time out for herself, expressing gratitude, getting plenty of sleep and taking pride in herself inside and out.

BADASS STANDARDS: GUYS, DATING, and RELATIONSHIPS

> Set your standards high and stick to them. People who want to be in your life will rise up to meet them

RULE #1
Teach men how to treat you: Set your standards and stick to them.

Why do some women always date really good guys, while others seem to date only the asses? You know, the guys that parents and friends *cannot stand* because he's such an ass? He stands her up, flirts with other women, criticizes her clothes, intellect, appearance—you know... a complete Tool.

There is a fundamental reason why this happens. It has nothing to do with physical attractiveness, money, intellect or status. Plenty of beautiful, successful women date men who treat them poorly. Plenty of self-proclaimed "average" women, date amazing, one-of-a-kind men. The types who treat them with kindness, respect, thoughtfulness and admiration.

The Secret: Set your *personal standards* and stick to them

The ability to consistently attract good people into your life, is not a magical power held only by select women. It is a power held by all women. It is the power to "teach" men (and people in general), *how* to treat you, by setting and sticking to your own, self-defined set of **personal standards**: *That is, the way in which someone must treat you, in order to be a part of your life.*

Badass women have learned, that by setting *personal standards*, they control *who* is allowed into their life and who is not. Those who don't treat them well, with the respect and kindness they expect—are shown the door. Simple as that.

Setting *personal standards* gives you the power to:

a) Control how you are perceived by guys.
b) Control the type of guy you attract.
c) Ultimately control how you are treated.

Whether it's casual dating, a long-term relationship or marriage—the power to define the people in your life, is yours and yours alone. Even if you've never tapped into your power prior to today—it is within you, waiting to be unleashed.

> **Like Glinda the Good Witch in Wizard of Oz said to Dorothy:**
> *"You've always had the power my dear, you just had to learn for yourself."*

More About Personal Standards

Personal Standards are your own set of life rules, outlining what is acceptable—and what is <u>not</u> acceptable to you when it comes to dating, relationships and marriage.

It is your "line in the sand" with respect to HOW you will be treated, spoken to, respected, loved and honored in a relationship. These are the minimum standards a man has to meet, in order to be in your life. I've also called personal standards—my Rules of Engagement!

For example, one of my "Rules" or *standards* if you prefer, was: *Must treat me respectfully and must speak to me respectfully.* This meant, the way a man treated and spoke to me had to *feel good*.

If he was condescending, needlessly critical, rude or didn't follow through on what he said he would do, I cut-bait and moved on. I had no interest in wasting my time trying to change behavior that runs *that* deep. People are who they are.

Another personal rule of mine, was not to accept a last minute date. (See RULE #2) For example, if someone asked me out on Friday, for a Saturday date, I always declined. If I was interested in the guy, I nicely said something along the lines of "Shoot—I would have loved to, but I have plans."

Even if I *didn't* have plans. Why? Because it was a subtle way of teaching him, that I was not a last-minute call. I have a life, and other things going on. If he asked last minute for a 2nd time, I said the same thing. Guess what happened the 3rd time? Yup. He asked me out a week in advance, and I accepted. I've now "taught" him how to treat me. I've taught him my Rules of Engagement for a date. Make sense?

> **Side Note:** Personal Standards hold true and apply to friends, colleagues, employers and life in general. However I'm addressing dating /relationships for simplicity.

It'll make your life easier and contribute to your badass confidence

Having clearly defined rules and standards may sound rigid, but I promise it will make your life much easier to navigate. It reduces the angst over "what to do" or how to respond, when most any situation comes up.

You'll also find that when you are clear in your *own* mind, that energy transmits loud and clear to others. People will sense in you, a tangible, bright energy of self-confidence, self-worth, value, assurance and strength, *and they will respond to you accordingly.*

Your Personal Standards List is living and fluid

Your personal standards list is meant to be *"living and fluid."* Meaning, they aren't set in stone, and you don't get just one-shot to make the list. As you grow and evolve, encountering different experiences, learning different lessons—add to the list.

The Purpose

Personal Standards act as a *powerful COMPASS* for the *forward progression and enhancement* of your happiness, well-being, goals, dreams, peaceful existence and overall life equanimity. They are not there to oppress and control. To the contrary, *they are meant to serve as a reference of the standards you feel will best serve you in life.*

My own personal standards are found in this section

This entire section on dating/guys/relationships contain many of my own Rules and Standards for relationships (when I was dating). My sister and I were blessed with amazing parents who instilled confidence and self-worth in us at an early age. This for sure, gave me a solid foundation on how I expected to be treated. Other rules, I added along the way from lessons learned the hard way.

Some, were based on watching the experiences of friends. You know—the times you see what a friend is going through and think... "Umm, there is NO WAY I will ever put myself in that position." There are a few of those in there too.

Whether you are 15, 25, 45 or 65+, my true objective is that you walk away with a nice handful of valuable take-aways to apply to your own life, or to help a young girl/woman in her journey. Everyone makes their own goofs, I mean—that's really how you learn . . . but if we can help each other navigate through the rougher waters, we are all the better for it.

> ## RULE #2
> **No one puts Baby in a corner! You aren't anyone's Plan B.**

Badass women are confident. They aren't anyone's last-minute pick. They aren't anyone's "Plan B." Who wants to be asked to the Prom the day before? No one!! Who wants to be asked out like this: "Hey, my first choice bailed for Saturday night, want to go?" No one!!

If you don't want to be seen as the "Plan B" girl... *Do not accept last minute date invites.* Even if you like the guy a LOT and have been hoping he'd ask you out. It sends the wrong message. I mean—if there's a huge sale at Nordstrom, aren't all the best items gone in a flash?! If you go on the very last day of the sale, you're picking from leftovers that no one else wanted.

I know it's a corny analogy, but you get the point right? The good stuff is swiped up first... YOU are a hot-ticket item, ergo—no, you are NOT available for a Saturday night date, if he asks you out Friday.

One of my personal rules, when dating—was not accepting last minute dates. Again, no one wants to be 2nd choice or "Plan B." If a guy asks you out on Thursday or

Friday, for Saturday night, you probably weren't his first choice. Or, he didn't think enough to ask you out well in advance, which to me signals *afterthought.*

In the event of a short-notice invite, it was politely turned down. My response was something along the lines of *"I would have liked to, but I have plans already."* Even if I didn't have plans, I still said I was busy.

I wasn't playing games, I was subtly communicating what *was* and *was not* acceptable to me. Not acceptable, is a last minute "hey my plans fell through, and I'll bet you're available" invite.

Guess what happened? Next time, he asked me out a good week in advance, with an increased level of respect and deference. Assuming I liked him, I rewarded the behavior with a "yes—love to." Now he knows the rules, and a baseline level of respect has been set. I trained our puppy the same way. Kidding-not-kidding.

IMO, if a guy sees you as a catch *(and of course we know you are!!),* he will ask you out *early.* It's not only respectful—but a "hot ticket" is bound to be booked up in advance. Right?

Creating value

In sales, we called this concept, *creating value.* **It goes like this:** Imagine there are 2 restaurants you are considering—neither of which you've been to before. For the sake of argument, assume the food quality it comparable.

Restaurant #1 is booked up *weeks* in advance, sometimes *months*. Every time you drive by—there's a line out the door of people patiently hoping to get in. If you want reservations, you'd better plan it in advance.

Conversely, **Restaurant #2** always has last minute reservations available. There's never a line outside, you can walk in at your leisure and pick any table. It's never more than half full.

SO... Which restaurant has a *perceived* higher value? Which one is more intriguing and holds a little more mystery? Aren't you dying to see what all the fuss is about with **Restaurant #1?** Of course you are. It's human nature. Billions of marketing dollars are spent trying to create buzz, intrigue and desire around products each year. Exclusivity, more demand than supply—all drive perceived value, and ergo—peoples interest!

Now obviously I'm not saying that as women, we are *products* to be sold or marketed. I want to make that clear. It was just an *example* to illustrate a point. My point is, it's human nature, human psychology—to place a greater *perceived* value on something or someone, that isn't a cakewalk to attain.

We really DO teach people how to treat us, through the *standards* we set, what we accept, what we don't accept.

Here is the BEST part for you:

IF you stick to your Standards, **you are FAR less likely to get into a toxic relationship in the FIRST place.**

Why? Because 9.9 times out of 10, the crappy guys will violate at least 2-3 of your Standards within the first 2-3 dates. Sticking to your Standards, and showing him the door, pronto—saves you time, drama and negative energy. Don't waste time on people who aren't worth it.

You will feel strong, confident, empowered and in control. That energy translates into the world. People will begin to react to you differently and treat you differently, in a highly positive way.

Also, the quicker you say "no" to those not up to your standards, the faster you'll attract the type of guy that deserves you. Promise.

RULE #3

Never chase a guy. Ever. If he's interested, he'll come to you.

If he likes you, he will make the first move. Resist the temptation to initiate. If you do, you run the risk of winning the battle but losing the war. In other words, asking him out first—may get you a first date, a relationship or even marriage if that's your end-game.

But here's the deal: In the end, guys like to feel that they "pursued and won you over." In other words, there was a competition and he prevailed. When you are the first initiator and the pursuer, *you relinquish your power*. The power dynamic changes from *you* as the decision maker and one-to-be-won, to him, as the one-to-be-won.

When the relationship goes through trying times, and believe me—it will, you want him to remember what a *challenge it was to win you over*. Guys place a subconscious higher value on something they had to "fight for", vs something that was pretty much there for the taking. I know this sounds super annoying to some, but IMO—that is just the way it is.

If you rationalize that he's "too shy" to ask you out . . . resist the temptation to take the initiative. The easiest way to go about this situation is pretty simple: Smile, be kind and receptive when he talks to you—basic things to make him feel comfortable.

A shyer type will probably dip his foot in the water by saying something like "we should see a movie sometime." Instead of saying, "Great! How about Saturday?" Instead, just smile and say "I'd love that!" Now he knows you are interested. Ball is in his court.

Believe me—I **KNOW** this sounds *really, really* archaic and it's not 1950!! This is especially cringe-worthy for those of us with very strong personalities, who have no problem asking for, and going for what we want professionally and in our normal day-to-day lives.

But what serves us professionally, and in the general day-to-day world, isn't always what works best for us *longterm*, with guys and relationships.

Keepin' It Real

When I was in 5th grade, I had a crush on Brian, a boy in my class. He was super cute, cool and an amazing Kick-ball player. You know, the whole package. I sort of thought he liked me too, and I really, really wanted him to pass me *the note* (you know the one): "Will you go with me? Yes ___ No ___ Maybe ___."

I was getting impatient! What the heck was he waiting for? Never one to back away from taking the initiative, I picked up the paper-list (no computers of course!), of the names, addresses and phone numbers of everyone in my class. It was actually for my mom, as a PTA member—but oh well.

My plan wasn't to ask him to "go with me." I at least knew not to do THAT. Instead, I planned to call under the guise of asking him about our homework assignment for Social Studies. I figured that might get the old ball rolling!

As I perched myself on top of the kitchen counter, I quickly scanned back to the "K's" (his last name), found his number, picked up our wall mounted avocado green phone, with the rotary dial and was about 3-digits in, when Mom walked into the kitchen. Seeing the look on my face—she immediately knew I was up to something.

"What are you doing." "Ummm ... calling Brian to ask about the Social Studies homework?" (I'm a bad liar—ask me a direct question, and I'll blurt out the truth.).

I will never forget what she told me: *"Put the phone down."* Click. I sheepishly put the receiver back. *"If a boy wants to talk to you ... He will call YOU. You do NOT call boys."* Crap. What a buzzkill.

But you know what—she was absolutely right. If a man is interested, shy or not, he will make it happen. That one small incident, over 30 years ago set the foundation for the way in which I approached dating for my entire adult life, including the way I met my husband.

Side Note: I am happy to report that Brian DID ultimately ask me to skate "Snowball" with him at the roller-skating rink a little while later. We held hands, while racing around the rink (me, trying not to bite-it) for a whole 3-minutes. Case closed. Thanks Mom!

RULE #4

When a guy tells you by his actions, who he is—*believe him*. The first time.

When you first start dating, that's when both parties are usually on their absolute best-est behavior. Right!? Aren't we usually all *extra* about being courteous and gracious, maybe a little extra accommodating in the interest of being a good sport? We'll put in extra effort to dress cute—especially for a date, do our hair, be extra nice to his friends, not critique his driving, etc.

For example, one time I agreed to a 5-day Snowboarding trip to Whistler, to impress a new boyfriend with my carefree-ness. First, I am not carefree. I plan and control everything otherwise I break out in hives. Second, I don't even know how to ski. I had been to a mountain once before, when I was 12. That one ended in disaster. Lol.

Guys go through the same dance in the beginning, as we do. They want to impress us too! The point is—everyone is on their best behavior in the beginning. SO—if early on, you see, sense or *experience* **Universal Red Flags**—*take heed.* **You are getting a peek behind his mask.**

Meaning, you are being blessed with a **foreshadowing** of who he really is AND what you can expect to experience more of in the future, should you continue the relationship.

I believe that when we are blessed with a foreshadowing, or a *peek behind the mask*, it is our spirit guides or our Higher Self, giving fair warning. It's up to you, whether to heed or ignore it. In my experience, if ignored, the price is paid later on.

It's so important to understand that. It can save you a lot of time and heart-ache. It is so much easier to cut-bait 6-*weeks* into it, vs 6-*years* into it. This is the perfect segue into a very important section that every girl and woman needs to be mindful of and watch for.

Whether you are just beginning to date, or are in a relationship or marriage, be aware of these 6 Universal Red Flags, that if present, translate to GAME OVER.

RULE #5

6 Universal Red Flags that translate to: GAME OVER.

Universal Red Flags are: Any behaviors, actions or attitudes that flat-out rub you the wrong way, leaving a bad feeling that you cannot shake. I call them *Universal* Red Flags, because they are *never ok* in a relationship. Or in general, for that matter.

You will *intuitively know* if you are in one of these situations, because it will resonate strongly within you—like the loud gong of a bell. If you find your *head*, trying talk your *gut* out of what your head is telling you . . . stop. The gut always prevails.

The (6) Red Flags to watch for are:

1. Disrespectful Words and Treatment
2. Lying, Deceit or Dishonesty
3. Volatile Emotions or Reactions, Controlling & Jealous
4. Wandering Eye or Cheating
5. Verbal or Physical abuse
6. Unreliable, Undependable, or Not true to his word

Let's take a closer looksey, shall we?

1. **Disrespectful Words and Treatment:**

    A *pattern* of biting remarks, searing words, hurtful actions or poor treatment which make you feel belittled, condescended, insulted, put-down, marginalized, unimportant, less-than, or bad about yourself are *disrespectful to you*. If you commonly feel this way around a particular person, that is your Red Flag.

    Letting a guy call you a bitch, stupid/dumb, loser, worthless, ugly, fat, or any other term that hurts, demeans, belittles or criticizes you is UNACCEPTABLE and a DEAL-BREAKER. No, I don't care if he was "just pissed off".

    If anything, saying those sorts of words to you in anger is a huge Red Flag that he does not have something that is extremely important, for a long-term successful relationship: **Conflict Resolution Skills.**

    Conflict Resolution, is the ability for 2 people to work through common irritations brought about by personal differences, misunderstandings, a hurtful situation or a disagreement, in a way that isn't hurtful or harmful to the other person.

    It's hard to stay completely calm—but people with strong CR Skills, will generally stay pretty centered, and seek to hear out the other person, state his/her side—but most importantly, seek a compromise or a solution that is agreeable to both.

In relationships, we're going to argue and get annoyed with each other on occasion. That's life. When Oliver (my husband) is being really, super annoying—I go into another room for personal space and to center myself. He used to follow me, because his personality is to resolve it right away. Whereas I need breathing room, and time to gather my thoughts and cool off.

What we DON'T do, is scream, throw things or hurl vicious insults at each other. In the 17 years we've been together, he's never, ever, called me a hurtful name—and vice versa.

If you are in a relationship with someone or in the beginning stages of a relationship with someone who puts you down as we've discussed above, my personal suggestion is cut-bait on the relationship and chalk it up to a life lesson that won't be repeated. You deserve authentic happiness in life.

People do *not* change that drastically. Reasoning, pleading your case, becoming upset, angry or emotional with the person, in response to a pattern of disrespectful words and treatment, *may* elicit an apology followed by a promise to cease the behavior—but unfortunately, *it isn't going away.*

You may even experience a pocket of calm for a period of time, with nicer, kinder behavior. Chances are, it is only a matter of time before it begins again. The smartest step, is recognize the situation for what it is, and get yourself out of it. THAT *is a badass move!*

2. Lying, Deceit or Dishonesty:

I use my visceral gut reaction as my litmus test. In other words, before a thought even enters my head—do I *feel* my body *respond negatively* or *take pause* to his/her words or actions.

For example, a little white lie to spare someone's feelings wouldn't cause me to take pause. I'd probably briefly notice, and without giving it much thought, think *"I'd say thing same thing. No reason to needlessly hurt someone's feelings, for something so small."*

On the other hand, things like knowingly writing a bad check, taking advantage of people, lying about weird things—would set off major alarms for me. Bottom line, if it is enough to make you stop and take note, and not in a positive way, chances are it is meant to be your Red Flag. Stop, listen and assess.

Keepin' It Real . . . my own story:

I started dating 24-year old CJ *(not his real name),* when I was 26. An athletic 6"4, with shiny dark hair, turquoise eyes and perfectly chiseled features, CJ had a larger than life personality. A charismatic extrovert, he was fun, gregarious, laughed easily, loved to go out on the town . . .

and thought I was the best thing since sliced bread. So—life did not suck at that point!

Having been in a rigid, intense relationship from the age of 17, CJ was a complete breath of carefree, liberating fresh air—and *that* was an addiction that would be hard to kick.

3-months into the relationship, I got my "Big Red Flag"

We were downtown at a hot spot for dinner. Per the usual, we arrived early to have cocktails. We were having fun, laughing, flirting and just enjoying the night. As the Hostess came to get us for our table, CJ asked the bartender for our check.

As he was standing at the bar, with his coat draped over the arm nearest the bar counter—I fortuitously looked down just in time to see him place his covered arm, over a pile of cash on the bar that looked to be payment from a previous customer.

Sleight of hand and twist of fate: In one fell swoop, like a magician—he swiped the money off the bar, into his hand and into his pocket. I was, in a word—*stunned*. I clearly remember my breath stopping, face freezing and mouth opening in disbelief.

He did not know that I saw. At the time—I was so shocked that *anyone* would do that, and was trying to process what had just happened, against the person I *thought* I knew.

I was brought up by amazing parents who instilled in my sister and me, very simple old-school American values: Tell the truth, earn an honest living, pay your bills, your word is gold, your family is the priority. To see someone I knew—*steal*, was beyond, beyond. I should have taken heed, and I did not.

I was given fair-warning, a foreshadowing, a peek-behind-the-mask, that this person was dishonest. I was shown *who* he was, and what I could expect *more of* in the future IF I continued the relationship. I ignored the waring, and continued dating him.

Yes, I was pretty young, but in reality—sometimes we have to learn things the hard way, and that's what happened to me.

We dated 4 more years, living together the last 2. During that time, I would catch him fibbing about the *weirdest*, most benign things. Things like proactively telling me he was "almost home", when in actuality he hadn't even left work *(and I wouldn't have cared either way)*. Or "I did legs at the gym today," when in reality he had done upper-body. I mean—just flat out weird things that no one, including me—would have cared about. It was bizarre.

Towards the end, the lying and dishonesty increased. We were living together, splitting utility bills and rent. The apartment and utilities were in my name—but he assumed the task of writing and mailing in the checks, while I'd write him one "large" check for my half of everything. Yes . . . this was before online bill payment. I feel very old now.

Odd things always seemed to happen in *our* apartment. Like, the lights would go out for, cough, NO apparent reason, cough. The cable randomly "wouldn't work." I had a weird feeling and would ask if he had paid the bills on time. Every time, he lied and said yes, but that he'd contact the cable/utility company and see what was going on.

I've heard it said, that if you don't *"listen to the whisper"*—the Universe will clobber you over the head with your lesson. And that's what happened.

After a particularly long day at work (I was an outside sales exec in a highly competitive industry), I parked my beloved light blue Honda Accord with the cloth seats and no air-conditioning, in my assigned parking spot.

As the warm elevator closed its doors and started humming its way up to the 3rd floor, I kicked off my heels, leaned against the elevator wall, closed my eyes—and smiled at the thought of a hot shower, my favorite cozy USD sweatshirt and curling up with a steaming bowl of Top Ramen. It had been a long day!

As I got off the elevator, facing my apartment door—I saw a white envelope stuck to the door. Hmmm? As I removed the envelope, I noticed the return address was a law firm. "What in the . . .?" I thought.

Unfolding the letter, at the top of the page in bold were the words "Notice of Unlawful Detainer." I didn't know what that was, but it didn't sound good. Reading the rest of the letter— I learned that I (we) *were being EVICTED from the apartment for non-payment.* Yes. Evicted. CJ had been depositing my checks, and not paying the bills.

Since the apartment was in my name, I am the one who had to go to the courthouse for a mandatory appearance. I don't remember "why", because honestly it was so long ago. What I DO remember with clarity, was the utter **humiliation** I felt.

Standing in a crowded courtroom in my black Ann Taylor business suit, with at least 20 other people who were obviously there for similar reasons was so humiliating, I cannot even communicate it to you. I gritted my teeth, clenched my jaw and just got through it.

I remember walking out of the courthouse to my Honda, thinking . . . "Never. Never. Ever, again... Will I put myself into that position. Ever. That's IT."

Here is the lesson: I was given a Big Red Flag, peek-behind-the-mask, fair-warning, 3 months into the relationship and I ignored it. Furthermore, I was given even bigger hints throughout the relationship of his proclivity to lie and deceive.

Still, I stayed. Finally, I got the clobber over the head in the form of a humiliating Eviction... which BTW, stays on your credit for a long time if I remember correctly. He ruined my credit at the time, of course.

I really don't know why I was so clueless, or why I chose to ignore what at a gut level—I knew was happening. I was in a relationship with someone who lied, stole and deceived—and I stayed. At least longer than I should have.

I know that everyone is going to make their own decisions. Sometimes we *do* listen to what others have experienced and change course. Other times we listen—but continue doing exactly what we intended to do in the first place.

Truth: At the time, had someone relayed this same warning-story to me, I probably would have continued down the same path, because I was stubborn and head-strong, to my own temporary demise.

That being said, I did learn the lesson. After CJ, you can bet that I DID heed early warnings thereafter. I'd cut bait and move on faster than you could say "cut-bait." I am positive, that I saved myself from reams of unneeded heartache, drama and negative relationships by doing so.

3. Volatile Emotions or Reactions, Controlling or Jealous:

Volatility is defined as *"liable to change rapidly and unpredictably, especially for the worse."* Examples such as unwarranted, explosive anger when driving, becoming highly agitated for seemingly small reasons, are clear signs of which to be mindful.

Same with jealousy and possessiveness. A healthy relationship doesn't cause one to feel constricted, controlled or isolated from life, friends and family. To the contrary. A healthy relationship encourages you to flourish and grow into everything you want to be.

A guy who is grounded, confident and secure with himself, will not attempt nor even *want* to control you. He is confident in what he has to offer and extends a natural level of trust and latitude in the relationship.

If something does not feel right, if there is a feeling of walking on eggshells, if you feel on edge, controlled or afraid to be yourself for fear of an outburst—that is a serious Red Flag, and candidly, I'd get out of the situation as quickly and safely as possible. No exceptions.

Where there's smoke there is fire. Volatility and jealousy can be very, very dangerous elements. At the very least, these emotions create a toxic environment of anger, distrust, anxiety, fear and tension in a relationship. That is no way to live. And, it is a Big Red Flag.

4. Wandering Eye or Cheating

Whether you are ridiculously beautiful or somewhere in between—we've all experienced a date or a boyfriend who constantly rubbernecks or flirts with other women, in front of you. I'm not talking about briefly noticing someone attractive—that's normal. We aren't dead—right?

I am referring to the guy for whom, it's perpetual. Almost like it is a part of his nature and he "can't help himself". That is not meant to be an excuse for him. Unfortunately, it's probably due in part, to insecurities that drive him to be what I call, a "BBD guy." A BBD, is the guy who is always on the lookout for the *Bigger, Better, Deal.*

Remember 4 things:

1. It has *nothing* to do with *you*, your attractiveness, dress size, job or anything else.
2. He will do the same thing *no matter who he is with.*

3. This issue is his alone, and he owns it.
4. When in doubt, refer back to 1-3.

If you've been dating for a little while, it's probably been a source of contention in your relationship. Chances are, it is a common argument whereby you become upset and somehow he turns the tables on you with statements like: "you're crazy (or) psycho," "it's all in your head", "you are insecure", or whatever the accusation.

I'll go out on a limb and say this: It is definitely NOT you. If the behavior sticks out like a sore thumb to you, *that's because it's happening.* It's NOT your imagination. It begs the question: If he acts inappropriately in your presence, what do you think happens when you are not there?

The most beautiful women in the world have been cheated on . . . So honestly, it is NOT a reflection on you. Please know that. My advice, is to move on. Don't let your beautiful self, get sucked into a relationship that hurts you, and makes you feel bad about yourself.

It inevitably turns into an extremely unhealthy cycle of hurt, anger, arguing—perpetually worrying about what he's doing, where he is, who he's looking at, checking up on him, spying—you know . . . Do you REALLY want to invest your precious, valuable energy babysitting a grown man? No! Badass women do *not* put up with bullshit!!!

Redirect your energy and amazing talents into positive things that propel you *forward!*

Keepin' It Real . . . my own story:

After high-school, I worked at Nordstrom for a couple years, before starting college. I worked at Store #1, the crown jewel, flagship store. It was a fast-paced, super fun, dynamic, downtown environment with lots of other young employees.

Kevin, (his real name, lol) a salesman in Ladies Shoes, had been after me for a long time, to go out with him. He wasn't my type, plus I had a boyfriend, so the answer was always "yeah, no."

He chased after me relentlessly for about a year, until he left Nordstrom for another job. A while after he left, I ran into him while grabbing a coffee. At that time, I was single (my boyfriend and I were taking a break) and he asked me out again. For whatever reason—I agreed. I don't know why. I think I felt bad turning him down so many times, plus I was single—so, whatevs.

The plan was dinner, then to The Onyx, which was the hot club at the time. Now you would *think* that after finally getting a "yes" from me, he'd want to be as charming as possible, right? Wrong. I got a whopping 3 Red Flags in the span of 1 date!

My first **Red Flag**, was the whole dinner experience. Looking over the menu, he asked me to split an entrée, ordered tap water only, was rude and demanding to the waiter, paid the bill with a check, then stiffed the waiter on a tip. At that point, his chance of a 2nd date was a big, fat zero. My thought was, get through the evening, then call it a wrap.

Next, we went to The Onyx to dance. While there, it was impossible to hold a conversation because he would literally crane his neck non-stop at every woman within a 20-foot radius. I wasn't annoyed because I liked him (I didn't), I was irritated at the complete level of rude disrespect.

It all ends on the dancefloor. Per the usual, the dancefloor was packed, which was super fun. Within minutes of getting to the floor, he turned his back to me and started "sexy-dancing" with a couple of other girls, leaving me pretty much by myself. Well, *he thought* it was sexy-dancing, frankly it looked like he was having a seizure.

At first I ignored it, thinking he may know them, or was just having fun. No big deal. Except it went on, and on, and on... with his back turned to me.

That was it. I had had enough. It was time for a badass move! I left the dance floor, marched outside, hailed a cab, cruised over to the next club where I knew friends would be and never looked back. His subsequent numerous apology voicemails went unanswered.

I ran into him a couple of years later at a popular bar. He tried embarrassing me in front of his friends, calling me out for ditching him on a date. He was short, so I said, *"Then all 5-feet of you should've been nicer to me, after begging for a date a hundred times."* I remember his friends cracking up at him. I know it was mean, but he asked for it.

In fairness, yes—cutting bait when you're treated disrespectfully is *much easier* when you aren't really attracted to the guy in the first place. So let's assume for arguments sake that I really liked Kevin, accepted his apology, and ultimately started dating him.

As months and (god forbid), years went by, the chances that our initial "bad date" was a complete and utter fluke on his part, are close to zero. Unless his body was overtaken by an evil entity—I got to see exactly who he was, and what the future would entail, if I moved forward with him.

We would have argued over his wandering eye, I would have become consumed with what he was doing, where he was, who he was with, whether he was lying about his whereabouts, etc.

In short, *that is no way to live.* It robs you of your life, happiness, growth and potential, like a blood-sucking parasite.

Red Flags are there for a reason. They are personal warnings from our spirit guides or angels, telling us to stop and take notice. The decision is ultimately up to each person individually, but the warnings are there.

5. Verbal or Physical Abuse

Verbal and Physical abuse is without question, an absolute and *immediate* deal breaker. Not the 2nd, 3rd, or 4th time it happens—the FIRST time. Here is how Wikipedia defines verbal abuse:

"Verbal abuse is when a person forcefully criticizes, insults, or denounces someone else. Characterized by underlying anger and hostility, it is a destructive form of communication intended to harm the self-concept of the other person and produce negative emotions."

Physical abuse, is causing intentional bodily harm to another, by actions including but not limited to kicking, punching, slapping, pinching or throwing.

Quite frankly, if you feel unsafe or even *uncomfortable* around someone you are dating or in a relationship with—that is NOT normal. A man laying his hands on a woman in anger—is unacceptable, not to mention a crime, punishable by jail and depending on the severity, prison time. That means . . . it is wrong people!! Get out as quickly and as safely as is possible.

To be clear, I am not a counselor, nor do I have professional first-hand experience with either forms of abuse. My input is based purely on common sense of what is right and what is wrong. It is *wrong* to intentionally hurt someone. It is *wrong* for a man to lay his hands on a woman in anger, period.

It is *wrong* to spew hateful insults, criticism, put-downs or destructive verbal behavior as a way of communication to anyone—let alone someone you supposedly love and care about.

If you are reading this book, chances are high that living a happy, fulfilling, joyful and peaceful life is important to you. If that is the case, ask yourself this simple question:

"Is the life I am currently living, leading me *towards* that goal, or *away from* that goal?"

If you answered "towards"—congratulations! You are on the right track. Continue listening to your gut, making decisions that truly serve your best and highest good.

If you answered "away from"—please know, that it says a great deal about your strength of character, that you're able to be honest with yourself even when the answer is difficult. Many people lie to themselves, to feel better, never resolving the obstacles in their path. You are ahead of the pack already.

If you are in the very nascent stages of a relationship, and have glimpsed of flashes of anger, controlling behavior, insults, criticism, physical aggression—get out safely and now.

If you are in an abusive relationship—the objective is to get out *as quickly*, and *as safely* as possible. Every person's situation is different, with its own set dynamics and variables. Enlist the help of family members or people you trust, to help find the right resources, licensed professionals and solutions to ensure that you are safely out of the situation, and out of harm's way.

You are a beautiful, unique ray of light in the world, worthy of goodness, safety, happiness and peace in your life. When you say "No," to people and situations that are not for your best good, the Universe will go back to the drawing board and bring you something better. That's the way it works.

6. Unreliable, Undependable, or Not True to His Word

A man's word has to be gold, if he wants to be with you. Dependability and reliability in a man is a non-negotiable. Meaning, if you can't depend on him to follow-through on promises, commitments and responsibilities, it's a deal-breaker.

It is a reflection on his moral character. It's also a clear message of the level of *respect* you can expect from him, in the future. Being able to rely on your partner, is a very basic, fundamental element of any relationship.

If he says "I'll pick you up at 8pm" . . . and he shows up at 9pm, that is unreliable. It's also disrespectful. If he says "I'll call you on Wednesday"—and he doesn't call until Friday, that's unreliable and disrespectful. If he agrees to pick-up your dry-cleaning as a favor, then blows it off—you can't depend on him.

You get the idea. Now obviously, unforeseen life emergencies or circumstances happen, whereby we have to cancel a date, we're running late, we legitimately, completely forget the dry cleaning, etc. *That's not what I mean, obviously.* If an emergency arises, and he's going to be late—call, and ask if it's still ok with you. That is common courtesy.

If he can't call on Wednesday—a quick text "so sorry—slammed today. Is it ok if I call you Friday instead?" Right?

At work—those who are unreliable and can't be depended upon, are fired. That's because it is important to the smooth operation of the business. Blowing off work, arriving late without a call, saying you'll do something then blowing it off—says "I don't care about the job, and I don't care if you fire me." Same thought-line with relationships.

Now, if emergencies and unforeseen events are fairly common, such that you immediately question if a date or plan will actually happen, or he'll actually follow-through on a promise, that falls under "unreliable."

Listen to your gut. Don't let your *head* talk you out of what your *gut* is telling you. If it doesn't feel right, and isn't sitting right with you—stop, assess and do what legitimately makes you feel at peace.

A good relationship offers a solid foundation of reliability and dependability in a world that can many times feel unpredictable. It should feel like a safe-haven. We all want to have people in our lives we can depend on!

Keepin' It Real

This is a funny story now, but at the time I was pretty ticked off at my parents for embarrassing me, lol.

It was in high-school, and I had always thought that Dennis, who was a year ahead of me, was really cute. Fun, athletic, and always the ringleader of getting Kegs for the parties—he was my kinda guy! At some point, he finally asked me out, and I couldn't have been more excited.

He was supposed to pick me up at a certain time—let's say 8pm, and we were going to a party where all our friends would be. I spent an hour and a half getting ready. A little before 8, my parents seated themselves in the living room ready to meet my date, as they always did. I joined them, and we waited for Dennis to ring the doorbell.

Side Note: Dates were expected to come to the door, shake hands with my parents, then sit in the living room so they could get to know him. Dad always asked what the plans were, then made it clear that I was to be home a few minutes before curfew (11pm). It always ended with Dad giving the guy an EXTRA FIRM handshake combined with direct eye contact. Lol. It's so funny to remember that.

8pm comes and goes, *no Dennis.* 8:15, 8:30, *no Dennis.* This is before cell phones, so . . . 8:45, 9pm rolls around—and I had fallen asleep on the sofa. I was so bummed. I had never been stood up and didn't like how it felt. Sad-face emoji.

Around 9:30—the doorbell rings. I leap off the sofa from a dead-sleep, rush to the door, happy he was there and ready to go! Dad beats me to the door and gives me the "I'll handle this" DAD look. Ahh crap.

I hear something to the effect of "Hi Mr. Nezat, I'm Dennis. Is Shelli here?" To my horror, Dad sternly asks him what time he was supposed to pick me up. I could hear mumbling about car trouble or something along those lines. Dad called bullshit.

In a nutshell, my dad told Dennis that if he tells me 8pm, he's expected to be there at 8pm. If he has car trouble, he should've called from a payphone. That aside, Shelli will not be going out with you tonight.

OMG!!!! Horrified!! I was ticked off with pretty much the entire situation. Bummed that I didn't get to go out with Dennis, mad at my dad for embarrassing me . . . then having to tell all my friends why we weren't at the party, and you know—the drama of being 16.

Point being—my parents were right. *They understood that it was teachable moment,* that would add to the foundation of self-respect and self-worth they worked hard to instill in my sister and me.

A woman/girl should never wait around, hoping the date shows up, ready to go when he feels like stopping by. Dad did exactly the right thing.

> **RULE #6**
> **Keep the values that make you feel strong—release all the others.**

Tradition. The word usually has a positive connotation, igniting memories of comforting times spent with family and friends. Traditions exist in our families, and they also exist in our culture as a whole.

Family traditions, like celebrating Christmas Eve at our house with broiled lobster, filet and martini's; opening gifts Christmas morning while my Grandma's famous egg-sausage-cheese casserole bakes in the oven; anticipating my Dad's Seafood Gumbo for Christmas dinner, are some of my favorite, most cherished family traditions.

Merriam Webster defines Tradition, in part, like this:

> *"The handing down of information, beliefs, and customs from one generation to another. The cultural continuity in social attitudes, customs, and institutions."*

Some of our *cultural traditions*, like the belief in honoring your word; treating others as you'd like to be treated, the thought that we are all created equal, entitled to equal opportunity are all positive top-level philosophies that we value.

That being said, a good number of these beliefs, while admirable, have not trickled down to include everyone in our society, as we are well aware.

"But it's tradition!" It's not always a good thing . . .

How many times have you heard someone exclaim with exasperation, "But it's tradition!" It's usually in response to something that was once acceptable, but as we grow and evolve as a society, we understand it is hurtful and marginalizing to others.

Considering the way women, people of color, different ethnicities, religions, or sexual orientation have traditionally been treated in our society, *tradition* by mere definition of the word—is NOT always a GOOD thing.

Choosing Your Traditions: Be thoughtful. Be mindful. Question + Assess

I am not suggesting a unilateral rejection of *all* tradition. Rather, careful reflection of those that in your mind, are questionable. Run them through your own filter, then decide if they stay in your life or they go.

I run "traditions" through this 4-pronged filter, before accepting into my life:

1. Does it contribute positively to my life, serving my highest good?
2. Does it enhance my life's happiness, growth, peace and long-term well-being?
3. Does it fall into alignment with my core values?
4. Does it promote acceptance, growth, happiness, peace, safety, equal access and well-being for OTHERS in the world.

For example:
Traditionally, women were limited to the home, while men enjoyed the power of career choice and head-of-household status. This tradition badly fails all 4 of my personal requirements.

Limiting the choice, access and financial power of a particular group, does not contribute positively to my life (#1). It would not enhance my happiness and well-being (#2). It does not fall into alignment of my core values (#3), nor does it promote the happiness, advancement or equal opportunity for *others (women)* in the world (#4). Ergo—this traditional belief is not accepted into my life.

There are however, two traditional values that I highly recommend and support: Chivalry and Waiting for Exclusivity. At first it may *sound* archaic—but hear me out! You'll find that both *contribute* to being strong, confident, empowered women.

Read on to Rule #7 and Rule #8 . . .

RULE #7

Expect CHIVALRY: It *does* matter . . . and NO it is *not* sexist.

Just as not all tradition is good, not all tradition is BAD or sexist either. I love and appreciate chivalry—whether it's a first date, 20th date—or 14 years into the marriage (my case). That means, acting like a gentleman and treating you like a lady.

> **Chivalry is all about respect.** I think of it as a modern-day tipping of the hat. It's a form of preferential treatment, respect, courtesy and in dating—the recognition that women are special, and our attention is to be sought, competed for and earned. It's recognition that we are "the buyer", and the buyer has choice!

It is NOT meant to infer that we are in any way, weak, incompetent, defenseless or helpless. Believe me—I've seen some of you ladies in the gym. I am *positive* that no man believes you are incapable of opening "that heavy door" all by yourself! Lol. He is being a gentleman!

A man's level of chivalry, or lack thereof—is one of the first things to note on a first date, and during the entire dating relationship. In my experience, *it is indicative of how he will treat you moving forward.*

Chivalry in a man, shows you his level of thoughtfulness, sensitivity, and his ability *and* desire to put you and your needs *first*.

Truth—would it bug you if your date swung open a door and marched through without holding it for you? Or if you mentioned being cold, and he said "Sucks for you! Glad I brought a jacket!" Or if the check came, and he pushed the bill over to you on a first date?

If these types of things would bother you, then chivalry is your game, baby. Own it!

Basic acts of chivalry to look for when dating:

- Opening/holding doors for you and for others as appropriate.
- Pulling out the chair to seat you.
- Letting you take lead when walking to and from, the table in a restaurant.
- Letting you order first.
- Planning dates vs "Hey. Wanna hang out?" So cheesy.
- Walking on the part of the sidewalk nearest to the curb.
- Offering his coat if you are cold.
- *Taking care of the tab.

*He should *always* take care of the tab on the first few dates. It's just the gentlemanly thing to do. It doesn't matter if it's just going out for FroYo—he should be courting you in the beginning. After that, it really depends on what makes you feel most comfortable.

For me, allowing the person I was dating to take care of the bill 100% of the time, crossed the line from "this feels good", to "I feel like a 12-year old child, hoping for an ice cream cone." So, I found a balance that seemed to work well: I'd usually let him take care of the tab for the first 3-5 dates, then I would make it a point to plan a little something and pay for it, every 2-3 times thereafter. I just went with what felt right at the time.

It seemed to strike a really nice balance between letting him be a gentleman and treat me, yet doing something nice for him, which as a side benefit, also made me feel strong.

But that's totally sexist!

No—it's not. Look, I'm fully aware that the idea of chivalry has been a **hot button** for a long time. There are some women who believe it is sexist, and in fairness—their argument has a degree of validity, if you consider it from a purely logical perspective. In part, they argue that chivalric acts are rooted in the idea that women are "weak," and can't fend for themselves, etc.

I've gone through this mental exercise myself, as I tried to navigate through the time we are living in, which is a very gray area when it comes to gender roles. Gratefully, they are no longer black and white. I say gratefully, because for women—it wasn't good.

You could be fired or denied a job for pregnancy, had to have your husband's signature in order to get a credit card (??), jobs in the newspaper were labeled "Jobs for Women," "Jobs for Men." I'm serious—my mom told me this. Jobs for Women of course, were all support positions. Men—managerial.

So, I can understand the confusion as we all try to navigate into a society where equal value is the desired norm. In doing so, *let's make sure that we don't throw the baby out with the bathwater.* In other words, some traditions still work, while others do not.

Let's just all relax and take a breath, shall we?

Paying women $.80 for every dollar a man makes, is sexist. Discounting her intellect, abilities, talents and contribution, based solely on gender, is sexist.

Opening a door, paying for the date, seating her first—is *not*. It is a level of courtesy that is recognized and greatly appreciated by the majority of women, in a world that seems to have forgotten how to treat others.

Chivalry does not make me, nor should it make you, feel "helpless," *(because we know we're not),* nor should it be taken as a sign that men think we can't do something. That isn't what they are thinking.

He is extending courtesies *because he likes you, wants to impress you* and wants to show respect. Just smile confidently and say, "Thank you!" Your strength and competence is exhibited in everything that you are—not in opening your own door on a date. Just sayin'.

I also didn't have an issue with male courtesies while in the corporate world. Gestures such as door holding and opening or letting me lead when being seated at a restaurant for business meetings did not bother me. I appreciated it, and felt it showed a level of taste and class in the man.

It did not make me look or feel incompetent or inferior, because I knew that wasn't the case. The ability to smile, say "thank you" and accept traditional courtesies such as these, is a subtle show of strength and self-confidence.

Consider this example of "The Rock" (yes, *that* rock):

I was watching a segment on the TODAY show one morning, while getting ready for the gym. The segment featured "The Rock." The Rock, whose real name is Dwayne Johnson, is an imposing 6"4, 250-lb, former pro wrestler, college football player—turned movie star action hero.

There isn't a weak or dainty thing about the guy. You'd assume he was there to promote another high-octane, butt-kicking, blow-everything-up, typical guy movie, right? Nope.

This imposing, force of nature was wearing an apron and oven *mitts,* showing one of the hosts how to bake his favorite chocolate chip cookies, while stressing the importance of using *real* vanilla. It was hilarious! Far from thinking less of him, I thought *more* of him.

He didn't have to brag about being confident, strong and self-assured. His ability to relax and not take himself too seriously, communicated his confidence loud and clear. He ingratiated himself to millions of fans, and undoubtedly won over new ones.

Conversely—imagine if the host asked him to bake cookies and he declined, scoffing about being too much of a bad-ass to bake. Wouldn't he look incredibly insecure, and in need of proving himself? YES!! You may even secretly think that his tough-guy image was a farce.

Likewise, when you are strong, competent and confident—graciously accepting little acts of chivalry *underscores* those qualities. You've just increased your perceived power!

Here's the kicker: Men *love* the opportunity to show off with a little chivalry! Watch them light-up like a Christmas tree when you notice and say, "thank you!" Whether it's the work-space or life-space, it makes them feel good and feel appreciated. That can only be to your benefit.

RULE #8

WAIT until he asks for *exclusivity*.

Yes—I'm talking about SEX, and yes I know it's not 1950 . . . but hear me out first. This one, little "tweak" solves so many common issues—you may change your mind.

> **Side Note:** If you're under 18—this is something to talk about with your mom.

If you think a guy is relationship material, and that is what you're looking for—WAIT until he has asked you to be in an *Exclusive Relationship*, before sleeping with him.

This is why . . .

— When you sleep with a guy outside of an Exclusive Relationship, *you shift the power dynamic from you—to him.* You ostensibly switch from the position of *buyer*, to *seller* . . . in a buyer's market.

— In his mind, he is free to have his cake and eat it too. Why wouldn't he continue seeing you and a few others? You can't cheat on someone, if you don't have an exclusive relationship, right? That is how men generally think.

— Not only have you relinquished, or at least diminished your leverage in the situation, but now there is an added layer of *extra-emotional attachment*, because you're sleeping with him!

I'd like to have a penny, for every time a single friend, sleeping with a guy she's dating, but not "Officially," said something like this: "I don't know if he's seeing other people, or just me. Do you think I should ask him? I'm so stressed about it!"

Or worst yet, she initiates *the talk*. You know, the one where she drills him on where the relationship is going, what he wants from the relationship, etc. . . . Now he's got one foot out the door, and thinks she's starting to get clingy and desperate. Not good.

By the time you have to ask a guy where he sees the relationship going—GAME OVER. It's a form of chasing, which is not an optimal spot to be in. Don't do it.

Make it easier on yourself. Slow your roll and wait. You have nothing to lose and everything to gain.

4 good reasons NOT to have sex, before an exclusive relationship:

1. **If he falls off the face of the earth, well, fine.** He didn't want a commitment and now you know sooner not later. You've smartly avoided the pitfall

of forming that extra emotional connection. This makes the healing process much quicker and less difficult. You will feel a little bummed it didn't work out, but that's about it.

2. **Waiting, provides you the mental and emotional mind-space to assess the relationship**, and what he has to offer, with much greater clarity. When that extra emotional connection is formed, we are more likely to overlook things we would otherwise "flag" as deal-breakers. *Waiting*, allows you to be much more objective, grounded and in control of the situation. That's empowering.

3. **It automatically and exponentially increases your stock.** You win either way! If he falls off the face of the earth, he does so remembering you with respect and admiration. If you *do* end up in a committed relationship—he will always remember that you had standards, and the confidence to stick to your guns. That can't ever be taken away from you.

4. **You *elevate* yourself above the pack.** Very, very few women take this tactic. You'll be one of the few, standing head and shoulders above the fray. The most important thing, is to feel proud, confident and powerful. This is exactly how you will feel, win, lose or draw.

Messaging

This probably sounds good in theory, but you might be thinking—"ok, but what do I actually SAY when it's crunch time?" I totally get it. Here are some FAQ's and Answers, below. I've included common situations, questions—and actual verbiage (from my own Playbook) you can use. It's not rocket science—but it IS helpful to see it first.

FAQ's

Q: When should I tell him?

> **A:** No need to make a big pre-announcement on a date or schedule "a time to talk" or anything formal. That would be weird. And awkward. Just enjoy dating and spending time together. When it gets to the "hot 'n heavy" point, stop and say:
>
> *"I don't do that outside of an exclusive relationship—and I'm not ready for one right now."*
>
> The reaction I experienced, was a semi-shocked to totally shocked look. Mainly because guys are not used to hearing that. Shock gave way to a whole new level of respect. I never got a negative reaction.

Q. But won't it look like I'm trying to manipulate a commitment from him?

A. NO. Specifically because your statement ends with "*. . . and I'm not ready for one right now.*" This very important part, makes it clear that *no decision* is needed or even asked for, at that point. Therefore—there is no pressure on either one of you!

Now he knows the rules! He'll go home and think about it. If he wants to be exclusive, he will proactively ask you later. If not, it'll fizzle out pretty quickly and you're better off moving on sooner rather than later.

Q. But what if I AM ready to be exclusive with him?

A. It doesn't matter. The objective is to communicate your standards, *without* putting him on the spot or creating an awkward situation. You DON'T want him to agree to exclusivity under duress (heat of the moment) just to get in your pants. That isn't the right way to start a relationship. Let him cool off, go home and think it through.

An added benefit in your favor, is that this also creates what in sales we called **"The Takeaway."** *The premise is: The harder you push someone—the more they'll resist.* The minute you "take it away" . . . . the more they'll want whatever it is you've taken away.

People want what they can't have, and guys like a challenge. You've ostensibly told him "Maybe. I haven't made up my mind yet." *That's the takeaway.* Unless he's really not interested in a relationship (which again, better to know sooner), mark my words—he will be back.

Q. Wonder if I make the statement, but then he still asks me to be exclusive *right then*?

A. He might . . . doesn't change anything. *Truth—my husband did this, lol!!* I had gotten out *"I don't do that outside of an exclusive relationship . . . and I'm . . ."* before I could finish he blurts out "I'M TOTALLY INTO THAT!!" (being exclusive), just as I finish *"not quite ready for that yet . . ."* Omg—I am dying laughing right now, remembering this.

Long story short, I said let's talk about it again tomorrow. I wanted to make sure *that I was ready* to be exclusive also. Needless to say, he called me the next morning, we went to dinner that evening—and he made it official. The rest is history. Drop mic.

RULE #9

Ending Relationships—pull-off the band-aid fast and hard. It's less painful.

The stronger and more confident you become listening to and following your intuition, the quicker you will know if and when it is time to end a relationship. This is true in both love and platonic friendships.

When you *know*, pull-off the metaphoric band-aid *fast and hard*. It will hurt for a second, but the healing process begins right away. Pulling it off slowly, hair by hair, will not only prolong the pain, it will delay the healing process and ability to get onto a healthy, positive, life-path.

Put another way, think of a breakup like an open wound. At first, the wound is raw and painful. If you leave it alone, it will heal in due time. If you keep picking at it, the healing process can't even begin. Only when you leave it alone, can the healing commence.

Focus first on wrapping up any loose ends, such as living arrangements, financials, or any other outstanding items. If you focus on this *first*, it will work to eliminate or at least mitigate, the need for on-going communication—so that the healing process can begin.

I get it—breaking-up is hard

It hurts. It's difficult. During the first stage, it feels as though the rug has been pulled out from under your feet, sending you free-falling through the Universe, not knowing whether or *if* you will ever land.

There is a hole where that person used to be, and you try to figure out how to fill it. Whether the relationship was toxic and awful—or you just grew apart and wanted to go your separate ways, it still hurts because it is a loss. It's like the old shoes that hurt your feet, but you sort of got used to the pain—and now they're gone.

Hurting and missing the person, does not mean you are meant to be together. It's just a normal part of the grieving process, when something or someone in your life is no longer there.

When this happens, most everyone has a tendency to hold-on longer than they should, dragging out the inevitable in teary, back and forth, on-and-off dramatic fashion.

True Story

> I had a friend, who after staying way-too-long with her boyfriend, finally broke up with him. We thought. What should have been a break-up, followed by time to heal before getting back to life, became a yearlong, drama-laden, never-ending-saga.

Why? Because instead of ripping-off the band-aid quickly, they pulled it off hair by painful hair over the course of a year. Neither allowed the wound to begin healing.

Frequent texting, nosing in on each other's Facebook or IG, casually getting together every once in a while—which sounds like a date, probably sleeping together every so often—became the new norm.

A little over a year past the initial break-up, she called me, devastated. He had met someone else. It was serious, and he asked that she not contact him anymore. Now, a year later, the healing process could start. The net result, wasting a year of her life, diminishing her power, losing her confidence and strength. Not good.

If it's meant to be, it'll be

Here's the thing ... If you're meant to be together, it will happen. There are true-life stories of breaking up, then later down the road, realizing you're meant to be together and the rest is history. Most of us are familiar with this cheesy, but true saying:

"If you love something, let it go. If it comes back, it's yours. If it doesn't, it never was."

Here is the take-away: You cannot miss someone, and someone cannot miss *you*, if there is not a complete break. Give the *time and space* for him to miss you, or you, him. Experience what life is like without each other. If it's meant to be, it'll happen. If not, I promise, the Universe has something much better planned for you. Have faith in the process.

Looking at it another way:

You're at a dealership, looking at a beautiful new car. The salesperson is all over you like a cheap sweater. You really want to be left alone, to experience and consider the car at your leisure, but he can't help himself. "It's a beautiful car! You'd be so lucky to have it! Should we get started on the paperwork?" he says.

Feeling overwhelmed and pressured, you leave. Over the next few weeks, you've enjoyed the luxury of personal time and mind-space to mull it over, and think about the car, without any outside noise. Final decision made, you are ready to move forward.

Keepin' It Real . . .

As I like to say, *"been there, done that, got the t-shirt, pen and a mug."* That's my way of saying, I have been down this road too! I know how hard it is. Here's my story . . .

I met my husband Oliver, at the gym. He had recently joined the gym where I had been a member for a few years. I noticed that he always made it a point to cross my path, nod and ask me if I was having a good workout. "Yes, thank you," was my response, as I moved on to the exercise.

As we both apparently worked out everyday—this became a daily ritual over the next 3 weeks. He finally walked over, extended his hand and introduced himself to me formally. "Hi I'm Oliver. I see you here all the time." (Umm, yeah, I know).

When he learned I was a runner, he exclaimed "Me too! *(he actually was not)* Want to go on a run this Sunday?" "Ok—sure," I said. Let's just say, the poor guy was *not* a runner, but he was a trooper. At 6"3, 220-lbs of muscle, running wasn't exactly his thang, lol. And yes, clearly I have *a type.*

We were running partners for the next 2 months. I was pretty sure he liked me, but he had not yet asked me out on a date. On a Sunday run, I had decided that if he did not ask me out at the end, I was going to cut-bait on the whole situation. I didn't need a running partner.

As the run ended, and I felt he had sufficient time to ask me (but had not), I said, "Ok—well, bye." "Wait! What are you doing next Saturday?" he said. "NOTHING!!" *I screamed in my mind!!* "Umm, I haven't decided . . ." was my outside voice answer.

He asked me to a movie, and we started dating exclusively a month later. Fast forward a year, he proposed on a weekend trip to Santa Barbara and we were engaged. It was an exciting time. He had just entered his 3rd year of law practice, and I was climbing the corporate ladder in Telecomm.

We were both busy, working and living life, so it wasn't until about 6 months into it, that I casually mentioned "we should probably look at setting a date." You have to know Oliver. Pinning him down to something he is either unsure of, or doesn't want to do, is like trying to pin a wave to the sand. He is my Artful Dodger.

If he doesn't want to give a straight answer, he'll say something along the lines of "Ok, that's something to think about," then skip to another subject, artfully avoiding both confrontation and commitment. He's a Gemini—what can I say?

This is how I discerned that, for whatever reason, he didn't want to set a date. *We would spend the next year, playing this cat and mouse game*—with my anger and frustration level rising. I was angry and hurt that he asked me to marry him, then proceeded to drag his feet.

As someone who is extremely decisive, operating best in "black" or "white", the dodging of a straight answer was so frustrating, I can't even tell you.

At the year and a half mark of our engagement, still arguing over a date, we had just moved into a beautiful new home. Sitting on the sofa one morning, looking around at the house that at one point in my life, I had only dreamed of having... I just felt... *sad*.

With great shame, I saw that I had turned into the type of woman I *never* wanted to be. A woman cajoling, haranguing and arguing with a man, to set a wedding date. I was embarrassed, ashamed and disappointed in myself.

I had allowed the situation to drag on. The only person responsible for my situation, was me. That is when the switch-flipped.

Women know what I'm talking about. That crystal clear moment in time, when you are DONE. The switch-flips, and there's no going back. It's an unemotional, practical decision.

Hasta la vista baby . . .

I grabbed my laptop, went to an online roommate site—and within 48 hours, found a place to live. Better yet, I was able to move in *that Saturday*.

I don't remember our exact conversation, but the gist, was that it was time we both moved on with our lives. I told him that I wished him a good life and happiness, but it wasn't going to be with me. I shared that I had found a place and would be moving out on Saturday.

Yes, there were protests and promises, but in short, I said *"It's not your decision anymore. It's mine."* I packed over the next few days. Saturday morning, I gave him a long hug, took-off my engagement ring, (ugh!!) placed it on the granite island—and left.

Pulling the band-aid off hard and fast . . .

The first night in my new place was the hardest. It was lonely, strange and I felt sick to my stomach with sadness. Over the next week, Oliver would call me sometimes during the day, but for sure every night before I went to sleep. It was hard on both of us.

It was comforting and familiar to hear his voice every night, but it was a crutch. My black and white personality, and natural decisiveness was the saving grace in this situation. I had decided to move on, and that meant cutting communication and contact, so we could both heal.

The last time he called, I explained that even though it's comforting to talk to him, it just keeps the wound open, making a hard situation, harder. I said, "I'm sorry to do this, but I have to ask you not to call me anymore." He respected my wishes, as I knew he would.

If it's meant to be it'll BE!

After that conversation, the healing process kicked in pretty quickly. Every day was a little easier than the last, and I started adapting to a new normal. I focused on work, spending time by myself doing things I enjoyed, and pretty soon started dating and having fun again.

I'm not one to cry over spilled milk, or lament over the past. What's done is done, and we can only move forward. Life is going to turn out the way it is supposed to, and I was confident that I would be given more, not less, if I just had faith in the process.

9 months later, it was a rainy Sunday

It never rains in SoCal—but when it does, it pours! It was Sunday, December 5th... You'll understand why I remember the day in a second. It was cold, overcast and raining. The wind was blowing so hard, the rain was horizontal. Being a Seattle native, I decided it would be a great idea to go for a beach run!

The beach was completely empty of course. No one was out. I ran 2 miles down the beach, then looped around to run back to my car. The very last leg of the run, is an incline, which is tough at the very end! As I'm looking down but slightly in front, I notice 2 legs running towards me. A slo-mo realization comes into my mind..."heeyyyyy....I know those legs..."

It was Oliver. The only other crazy person, who would go for a beach run in a storm. I raised my hand, expecting to smile and wave hello as we continued on our own respective runs.

Instead he suddenly stopped, removed his hat, wrapped his arms around me and buried his face into my neck, breaking down in tears. I didn't know what to do, other than put my arms around him and ask if he was ok.

Through sobbing tears, he choked out that he had made a terrible mistake, everything went wrong after I left, and he had F'ed it up and now I was gone. Oliver is *not* a crier, so I knew that he was in turmoil. I instinctively felt that he wouldn't be able to move forward anytime soon, unless he had final closure with me—and I wanted to give him that gift.

With that in mind, I offered to get together during the week. I wanted him to feel heard, and I wanted him to move on with a light heart.

Your life can literally change for the better in an *instant!*

Here's the exciting, awesome thing about life. One minute you're walking down the street feeling a little bummed or meh. The next *second* you turn the corner and in an *instant*—life completely changes for the better!

That's what happened, quite unexpectedly I might add. Oliver asked me over to the house, to talk. I went over on Wednesday evening, 3 days after our Sunday beach encounter. My intention was to listen and help him to feel a sense of closure. I wanted him to move-on without a heavy heart.

I gave him a hug, asked if he was feeling better, and sat on the sofa. He took out a very long, handwritten letter and started reading it to me.

The contents are for us (I keep that letter in the Safe), but it was something from the heart, and it moved me. In short, he took responsibility for what had happened, and shared with me what he had learned and thought about as he went through 9-months without me in his life.

The time he spent alone, allowed him to grow exponentially and reflect upon what he wanted, what was most important in life. At the end of the letter, I was speechless—which doesn't usually happen, lol! I was not expecting this! Finally I said, "So...I'm not sure what you want from me?" He wanted to get married. Period.

He had a few hoops to jump through, to mend the fences with my parents (particularly my dad), who were very hurt over the whole situation. He rose to the occasion, as I knew he would. The lawyer in him, presenting an air-tight case, came out in full form, and all was well again.

We eloped!

Three weeks later, on December 30, 2004, we went for a morning run on the beach, ate breakfast at our favorite spot, jumped in the car and drove up to Santa Barbara to get married.

We had a martini in the room as we got ready, and a Justice of the Peace met us in the lobby of the Four Seasons Biltmore, where we were staying. We walked outside, where I pointed to a pretty spot on the grounds and said "this looks good!" He married us right there, as we both read our vows.

It was great! Afterwards, we had drinks and dinner at the Biltmore with friends who lived in

Santa Barbara. We stayed for the week, and just enjoyed *being*.

That's our story. He needed time to understand life without me. I needed to honor my sense of self-worth and self-respect, by leaving a situation that was not (at the time), for my best and highest good.

It was vital, that all communication was broken. I had no intention of seeing him again. For me, it was over and I wasn't looking back. As a matter of fact, I was dating someone when we ran into each other on the beach.

Here's the take-away: If it's meant to be, it'll happen, but don't count on it. When it's time to leave, leave. Break communication as soon as possible and move on. One of two things will happen: 1) You'll get back together. 2) Something much, much better is in store for you.

Either way, when you listen to and honor intuition, it always serves you.

> ## RULE #10
> **Watch how a guy treats his mom. The way he talks about her, to her, and treats her—is indicative of how he feels about women in general, and is indicative of how he will treat you.**

Badass women by definition, have a strong sense of self-worth. She values herself, is confident in what she has to offer and *knows* she's a catch! Because of this, she expects the man in her life to treat her in ways that *underscore* these beliefs.

Whether it's casual dating, a long-term relationship or a marriage—being treated with kindness, respect, thoughtfulness and admiration from the man she is with, *is a non-negotiable.* Meaning, it's a *must* and something on which she will not compromise.

When we first start dating someone, we are all on our best behavior! If you're starting to think long-term about the relationship, have you ever wondered if he'll continue to treat you just as well, as the years go by? Wouldn't it be awesome if you could predict how a guy is going to treat you for the long-term?

While no one has a crystal ball and there are exceptions to every rule, if you want a good indicator of how he will treat you, *look at how he treats his mom.* A guy's relationship with his mom has *a lot of influence* on how he will view and treat the women in his life (you!) and women in general. It's virtually impossible for a man to treat *you* like gold, and every other woman outside of your relationship—like dirt. It's not plausible.

We give to others what we were given ourselves. Take a good look at the relationship he has with his mom. How does he talk about her? How does he talk *to* her? How does he treat her? Is he kind, helpful, caring and respectful to her? These are really important things to note, my friend, because . . .everything comes home to roost.

Here are 4 things to watch for, in his relationship with his mom:

1. Kindness and Thoughtfulness

So key! Does he proactively jump in to do little things to make her life easier without her asking? Like carrying groceries or her suitcase in from the car, or asking if he can get her something from the kitchen? Does he do thoughtful things to make her feel special and cared for? If yes, this is a guy who will be thoughtful of your feelings, treat you with kindness and look for ways to make your life easier and nicer. He'll take pleasure in making you feel special!

When Oliver's (my husband) parents us visit from England, he always insists on picking them up from the airport even though he could just send a car. He carries their suitcases up to the guestrooms, makes sure they have fresh towels and toiletries—then makes his mom's favorite cookies to have with her tea. He shows the same level of kindness and thoughtfulness to me. If I'm out of town, he will text me the day I'm due home and ask what he can get me from the grocery store. When I get home, he has my favorite foods all stocked in the fridge and will even run me a hot bath. Point is—it is the same level of thought and kindness he shows his mom. Watch for it!

2. Respect—Verbal and Non-verbal

I've found this one to be really important. Respect is both verbal and non-verbal. It's in the way he speaks *to* and *about* his mom. Does he speak highly and respectfully of and to her? Is he respectful and gentle even when he disagrees? If he speaks to her harshly, that is a Red Flag! Don't ignore it. Run, don't walk!

When she's talking, does he listen and look her in the eye, or does he look annoyed, dismissive, impatient and generally give the impression that whatever she's saying is unimportant? Respect is one of those things that you just know it when you see it. It either feels good, or it feels belittling. Honor your gut. You can bet that a guy will show you the same level of respect (or not) that he shows his mom, pretty quickly in the relationship.

3. Love and Affection

How affectionate is he with his mom? Does he give her a hug when he sees her, or is he cool and stand-offish? Do you sense a general level of love, warmth and genuine affection between them or does there seem to be some distance? If he doesn't show warmth and affection to his mom, chances are it'll be the same with you. If you're just starting to date, you may not see it right now, but as time goes on chances are high that his level of expressing love and affection will dissipate.

4. Listening to Her Opinion with An Open Mind

Respect is shown just by listening with an open mind, giving weight to her opinion because he values and respects it. Ultimately he makes up his own mind. After all, if he does *everything* his mom says—you've got a mama's boy which is a whole different conversation, but listening with an open mind shows a general predisposition towards respect for a woman's opinion. You want that! If he's dismissive right off the bat, towards any of her opinions or suggestions—guess what? He probably isn't going to give your input much weight down the line, either.

If he is Close, Not-too-close, or Dislikes his mom

Close: If his mom was warm and nurturing

If his mom showered him with love, kindness, affection and respect growing up, chances are, he'll express these nurturing behaviors towards you too. A guy who has a close and loving relationship with his mom, has a much easier time developing the same kind of relationships in his love life. It feels natural to him!

Not-too-close: Minimal love and affection

Guys who experienced minimal expressions of love and affection by their mom's growing up, can feel uncomfortable giving and receiving love and affection to their partners. It feels like foreign, unchartered territory for them.

It isn't that they won't have respect for women in general (they do) and be able to enter into relationships with them (they can). It's that once the relationship starts getting serious, they'll get scared and will sometimes create problems to end the relationship, retreating back to their safe-space.

It might be a bit more challenging getting him to open up to you, but it isn't impossible. It will just take a bit more work from your end, so the question is whether it's worth the time and effort on your part.

Dislikes: If he really doesn't like her

If he really dislikes his mom, **beware.** It is a toxic relationship waiting to happen! Mom's who are, or were abusive, withheld love, care, kindness and affection—create incredible damage on a child, male or female. A man who grew up under these circumstances ends up being disrespectful and resentful towards women, as an adult. In a relationship, they do what they can to cause pain, mental or physical. Sort of like venting, when you've had a bad day—except worse. They lump women into one big box labeled "no good".

These are the guys who are disrespectful to women close to them *and* women who are mere strangers. Ever had a guy get unusually angry and insulting because you turned him down for a date or didn't want to talk to him? Chances are, he fell into this category. If you are involved with him, he's the guy who seems to enjoy hurting you and tearing apart your confidence and self-worth. *In short, these are men who you will end up having toxic relationships with—IF you stay. Don't.*

Don't be a martyr, thinking he has such great "boyfriend" potential and you're the one to help him. The only thing that happens, is you get hurt, demeaned and betrayed time and time again because he doesn't know how to love in a healthy way. You can't be the one to change him. Coming to terms, working through and making peace with his past takes time and personal commitment to work that he has to do on his own. *That's not your role.* Wish him well and move on.

The mom and dad factor—watch the way his father treats his mother

I love this one. In my own experience, it has been 100% true in EACH of the 4 main relationships I've had in my life, including my husband. Without exception, the way the dad treated the mom, was almost exactly the way the guy treated *me*.

The way a guy treated me, tended to be a combination of his relationship with his mom, and the relationship dynamics between his parents. Think about your own current or past relationships as well—do you see a common thread?

I've heard it said that the biggest influence in a child's life, is the same sex parent. It would then stand to reason, that a man would naturally model his treatment of women, after his father and the way in which he saw him treat his wife (the mother), growing up.

I know it isn't always fair. We don't get to pick our parents. If a guy had the misfortune of growing up with poor role models and now visits those poor behaviors and attitudes on you, your kind soul may feel compassion and a desire to "help him" through it.

My advice is this: It's not your cross to bear. You weren't put on this earth to be someone else's dumping ground, for the sins of the parents. It's up to him to get the professional help he needs *before* entering into a relationship. There are lots of fish in the sea—get a healthy one!

Take-aways

Pay attention to the way he treats his mom, and also to their relationship overall. If he is kind, warm, loving and respectful to her, speaks highly *of* her and *to* her, listens to her opinion *and treats you the same*, then you've got a keeper!

If he and his mom have an unhealthy relationship, he speaks disrespectfully and poorly *of* her and *to* her, run. Any man who is disrespectful, rude and unkind to his mom isn't going to have any qualms treating you the same way.

BADASS
LIFE FUNDAMENTALS

> Be the kind of woman that when your feet hit the floor each morning the devil says "oh crap, she's up!"

RULE #11

Live by the 10/90 Rule: Your life is 10% *what happens* to you, 90% *how you handle it*.

Badass women take action and responsibility for their own lives. She knows she's the creator and master of her own happiness, her own life trajectory. She looks at the cards that were dealt, then quickly builds bridges and boats to get to where she wants to go.

She understands the 10/90 Rule:

Your success in life is 10% what happens to you and 90% how you handle it.

What happens to you, is the hand you are dealt at birth, life challenges and experiences. *How you handle it,* are the ways in which you react and respond. In other words, the way you handle life's challenges and adversity.

Think about how empowering this is. It means that regardless of the hand you were dealt or the challenges that arise—the power to change the trajectory of your life moving forward, lies within *you*.

Why are some able to rise-up in the face of great adversity to lead positive or even extraordinary lives, while others fall victim to the same circumstances? How is it that one person, born with great advantage and opportunity will squander their life, while another born with cards stacked against them will rise-up and thrive?

The answer lies, in *how each person reacts to the cards they've been dealt.*

Consider the two scenarios below. The first, *Silver Spoons*: Some, who were given great advantages and opportunities, yet squander them. The second, *Wrong Side of the Tracks*: Some, born with the cards stacked against them—turn lemons into lemonade, creating extraordinary lives. Why does this happen?

Read, then reflect on people you may know who fit into each category:

> **The Silver Spoons:** These fortunate ones are born into lives where they are afforded great opportunity and advantage. Well-educated, well-connected parents with financial resources, the best schools, tutoring, fully paid college educations, healthy bodies, smarts and a strong family structure to lean on.
>
> One would naturally surmise, that these kids are going to go far in life. After all, if someone starts at

mile 13 of a 26.2 mile marathon—won't they win the race? Not always.

I can think of many examples in my own life, where *some* of the Mile-13 kids (those starting at the halfway mark of life's marathon) squandered this incredibly advantageous position, choosing not to capitalize on what they were given or even worse, self-sabotaging. I call this "peeing on your own cornflakes."

In short, despite the advantages and leg-up (10% what happens to you), they ended up doing very little with their lives and felt like failures (90% how you handle it).

The Wrong Side of the Tracks: These types were born into difficult circumstances, and great adversity. Perhaps they grew up impoverished, had a dysfunctional family structure, little support, and weren't afforded education or higher education. Maybe they were born with physical challenges or extraordinary life events that would have stopped most people in their tracks.

Despite the obstacles and in spite of the odds, they consistently turn lemons into lemonade, leading extraordinary, happy, fulfilling lives. These types never see themselves as victims, at least for long, because they're too busy finding another way through the door.

In part, what generally separates those who consistently overcome obstacles, from those who don't—*is an intrinsic knowledge of their own internal power*. That is, the power of choosing how to respond to adversity, in ways that propel them forward in life, not back.

They understand the 10/90 RULE:

Life is 10% what happens, 90% how you respond.

How would you respond to these (3) typical Life-Challenges?

1. **What Happens to You:** For a 3rd time, you were unfairly passed over for a promotion.

    How Do you Respond?

    A. Stay. Continue to feel resentful and frustrated.

    B. Accept that the company is no longer a fit for you. Put feelers out, secure a position elsewhere with opportunities aligning with your goals.

2. **What Happens to You:** You're in an unhappy relationship. Feeling constantly disrespected and unimportant, numerous attempts to communicate

your feelings and rectify the issue have fallen on deaf ears.

How Do you Respond?

    A. Stay and be a victim. Continue complaining to friends, family and the person in

    B. Go. Chalk it up to a learning experience. Confidently understand what to look out for next time and avoid it. Reclaim your own happiness, redirect your life.

3. **What Happens to You:** You really want to buy a home, but it's so expensive. Under your current lifestyle, saving enough for a down-payment will take forever.

   How Do you Respond?

    A. Accept that this is your lot in life, and home ownership isn't possible. It's for other people, not for you.

    B. Decide you're going to do it. Put together a plan. Cut out unnecessary:
   — expenses, transfer that money into savings each month. Work
   — extra hours, work weekends, accept small projects to accelerate
   — savings. Build your nest-egg and make it happen over time.

In each case, you can see how life trajectory is determined by *how we deal* with challenges—not the actual Challenge itself. Think about how choosing response A or B would shape the course of one's life.

Choosing "A" in all 3 situations, would lead you down an entirely different road, than choosing "B". Now multiply that theory all the way down to *daily decisions*, and you'll begin to appreciate the immeasurable power and control we have over our own lives!

Overcoming the emotional hurdles

I think the hardest part of Life Challenges, are the *emotions* that come along with them. The way we feel is so powerful to our level of motivation and desire to take positive action. It can feel depressing, hopeless, frustrating and angering.

We have 2 Cavalier dogs—Emma and Logan. Logan's favorite thing in life, is to sit perched atop the back cushion of the sofa and watch everyone. Last week, I couldn't find him for about 20 minutes, which is concerning since he follows me everywhere.

Looking at the sofa, I noticed the cushion-back falling slightly forward. I walked over, and quietly wedged deep down in-between the cushion and back of the sofa, was Logan, looking at me helplessly with big brown, sad eyes. He had quietly resigned himself to his fate, immobile and squished between the sofa and pillow.

Like Logan, everyone gets wedged between life's cushions from time to time. And like Logan, sometimes we are tempted to resign ourselves to our perceived fate, because it feels overwhelming at the time.

When this happens, remember the 10/90 rule and take action

What's happened, has happened. Now the ball is in your court. *This is your 90%.* Begin by writing down (yes, on paper) an informal list of every way you can think of, to handle or respond to what has happened.

Do not censor yourself! Just write. Write whatever options come to mind—both positive *and* negative. It will feel cathartic to get it all out.

Next, look at your list. Categorize each idea under one of two columns labeled: *Forward Moving* or *Stagnant.*

Forward Moving options, are those that propel you forward in a positive way, in ways big and small.

Stagnant options, are those that keep you exactly where you are in life OR will have a negative, backward effect.

Focus on your Forward Moving list. Unless you feel otherwise, start with the *smallest or easiest option first.* Why? Because you eat an elephant one bite at a time. Meaning, big challenges are met not with an immediate turning of the Titanic, but rather with a series of one, *doable* step at a time.

Just a *tiny* step forward will ignite within you, the spark and excitement of forward inertia. You'll be amazed at the jolt of confidence, that a little taste of success injects into your soul.

And little successes, spark bigger successes!

Keepin' It Real . . . my Mom and Dad

As with most of my writings, it is through personal experience not pontification, that I offer perspective and guidance. I don't believe in preaching from Ivory Towers. If I'm writing about it, chances are I've lived it.

The *10/90 Rule* is no exception. It has been one of *the* biggest factors in my life, and one of the largest influences in my belief system. God puts certain people into our lives, to help us learn lessons necessary to our souls evolution and growth. Sometimes the people are difficult and hard, other times they are loving, inspiring and amazing.

My sister and I were blessed with two parents, who are the latter. Loving, caring, generous, selfless, amazing people with a solid value structure and priorities clearly in place.

My parents are rooted in refreshingly simple, basic, values: The happiness of their marriage and each other, the happiness and well-being of their daughters, truth and honor in your word, honesty and candor even when difficult, standing your ground, accountability, responsibility, apologizing when you've needlessly hurt someone.

As grown adults, I like to believe that we are blessed with a greater sense of clarity and understanding for our parents, their struggles and how difficult some things must have been on them. You can't truly appreciate that as a child.

As an adult, when I reflect upon where my parents came from, the immense challenges they faced individually and as a couple, to where they are today—it is *impossible* to deny the power of, "Life is 10% what happens, 90% how you respond."

They had every objective reason to say "I can't because . . ." Instead, they said "We can . . ." And they did.

My dad had every reason to be a victim of, "What happens to you"

Born the 7th of 11 children in the tiny, deep south town of Port Barre, Louisiana, it was a very hard, impoverished life for the family of 13. The family lived in a 1-bedroom shack without plumbing, and an outhouse out back.

To put food on the table, the entire family picked cotton in the fields from early in the morning until late at night in the blazing hot Louisiana sun.

Dad says that although it was coolest in the morning, which is why they started early—it was backbreaking work because the dew would settle into the cotton, making it extra heavy in the sacks they carried on their backs.

Dad had to quit school in the 8th grade, in order to work the fields and help the family survive. Poor, disadvantaged, with an 8th grade education, *on paper* there was every reason to believe this person should not succeed. He would have had valid reason to preface most every sentence with *"I can't because"* But that isn't my dad, as you will see.

He would later tell me, that he always knew on some level, he wasn't supposed to stay in the small town. Now, it was a matter of grabbing opportunity when it knocked. And it did . . .

At 17, fate intervened

A military recruiting officer had come to the tiny town and set up a small table at the local community hall, with brochures to join the military. Word spread quickly that "someone new" was in town, and Dad went down to check it out. The officer explained that he'd get to travel on a ship while serving his country—and if interested, Dad should go to the recruiting office in Opelousas, which was about 9 miles away. A *long way* on foot!

Bingo. This was his opportunity. He knew it, *and he took it.* Without a car of course, he hitchhiked to Opelousas, took the exam on site, passed, and enlisted with the United States Coast Guard.

2 things stood out to me when I first heard his story. 1) How was he able to join at 17, when you had to be 18. 2) How was he accepted without a high-school diploma.

He forged his father's signature of approval. As for the high-school diploma, he doesn't recall how that was overlooked, but I chalk it up to his angels working overtime, to set him on his way.

Fate intervenes again—he meets my mom

At 17 years of age, Dad was enlisted with the Coast Guard, assigned to travel various parts of the world on Ice Breakers.

At age 20, the hand of fate would gently steer him left instead of right, and he would meet my mom. Dad was stationed for a short time in Seattle, WA. He received orders to report for duty on a particular ship. At the requested day and time, he grabbed his Seabag, and reported to the ship for duty. No sooner had he gotten settled into his assigned barrack, then another Seaman poked his head in—"Hey Nezat—you're reassigned to the Winona", another ship at the same docks.

With a shoulder shrug, he picked up his stuff and walked across to his new ship. Walking up the ships plank, another seaman smiled and introduced himself—"Don." They were immediate friends, along with a crew of a few other troublemakers I'm sure.

A few months down the road, Don got engaged to his girlfriend, Linda, and asked my dad to be his Best Man. At the wedding, my dad noticed the cute Maid of Honor... my mom! That is how they met. He asked her out, and she told him "no," she had to wash her hair!! Lol—I'm serious.

He asked again, and they went out for grape soda. 6-months later, at age 20 and 21, against my grandparents wishes—they were married.

Side Note: Mom and Dad are still besties with Don and Linda to this day. We grew up with their kids. Mom, Dad, Don and Linda go on cruises together, always stay in touch and visit each other as often as possible. I love that!

Honestly, when I look at pictures of their wedding day, they look like babies. Of course my grandparents had good reason to be concerned. Their 20-year old daughter, marrying a military man who wouldn't be able to spend much time at home. *On paper* it was a recipe for disaster.

In reality, they were meant for each other. Both pulling out strengths in the other, to make a stronger union and stronger life.

Building something from nothing

A number of years later, the clouds parted, the angels sang, and . . . .into the world I was born! 18-months later, my sister came along and now we were 4.

When I was 3, we were transferred from Seattle to Huntington Beach, CA. We were a very young military family, with literally (as Mom tells), $0.05 cents left over at the end of each month after the bills were paid. That's 5-cents. Not 50-cents, FIVE-cents. A nickel.

In Huntington Beach, we were assigned to military housing, which are government owned and subsidized housing units for military families. As Mom tells the story, she and Dad walked into our assigned unit, and her heart sank. It was dark, dank, smelling of cat urine. The floors were filthy dirty peeling linoleum, dirty walls with crayon scribbles throughout from the last family, and overall—in a state of disrepair.

Mom, who came from extremely humble beginnings herself, wanted more for her girls. She and Dad stood still in the middle of the unit, in complete silence. They were very young, with 2 little girls, living on an enlisted-man's salary... and they knew it was all they could afford.

At that point, there were 2 choices: Accept the cards they were dealt OR figure out another way.

Here's where the 10/90 Rule comes in:

— 10% = It was all they could afford. (What happens)
— 90% = It was all they could afford *under the current situation* (How you respond or react).

Mom said, "I'm not raising our girls here. Let's go home and figure something out." So they did.

They figured out how much they would need for a modest, non-military rental. They also wanted to be able to save for a home of their own someday. Dad's military salary wasn't going to get them there.

If they *wanted* different, they needed *to do* different.

Here's what they did:

— During the day, Mom cared for neighborhood children (informal day care).

- Dad worked full-time with the Coast Guard, as usual.

- He took a 2nd job at McDonalds, from 6pm-12am, Mon-Fri. That meant he had 30-minutes to eat and change, in between jobs.

- We had 1 car (a VW Bug). At midnight, Mom put my sister and me in the car, to go pick up my dad after his shift. Even though I was 3, I have a clear memory of pulling up to the drive-in McDonalds, and seeing Dad in his McDonalds white uniform, with the white hat, wiping down the steel countertops. At midnight. He always brought us an ice cream.

- On weekends, Mom worked as a cocktail waitress.

Between the two of them, they worked 5 jobs. Coast Guard, McDonalds, Day-Care, Cocktail Waitressing, full-time mom. We were able to live in a modest, clean home with a neighborhood full of nice families and other kids to play with.

That would have never happened, had my parents said, "We can't because . . ." They figured out another way.

Their next 10/90 move

A few years later, they had a down-payment to buy my grandparent's house, in Seattle, WA, my hometown. The house, built in 1911, was built to serve as a Room & Board house. The main level and basement was where our family would live. The 3rd floor, housed 5 small rooms, with one shared bathroom for Boarders to rent.

The market value of the house, would be very tight for my parents. But, Mom calculated that if she rented out the 5 upstairs rooms, plus Board (providing meals), that money would generate enough to cover the bills *and* put money aside for their other goal—which was buying a rental property.

They schlepped all around town, trying to get a loan. Ultimately, the banks wouldn't approve them for the amount needed. Here's the 90%... Instead of accepting *what happened*, they *responded* by creating a resourceful plan with my grandparents:

On paper, grandma priced the house to match the loan amount that the bank *would* approve for my parents. They then bought the home for market value, writing 1 check each month to the bank, and a 2nd check to my grandparents who carried the loan balance.

We moved in, and Mom set up the Room & Board and started filling the rooms.

Scrappy, scrappy doo. Next goal was to buy a rental house

My parents had also set a goal, to buy a rental property. They intuitively knew (at 25 years old?) that they had to find a way to create a *passive revenue stream* that would support them during retirement. Rental property felt like something they could do.

My mom generated income by running the Room & Board, 6-days a week, while raising my sister and me (Dad was out to Sea quite a bit). It was not a walk in the park. The "Board" part, meant that we cooked and served Breakfast, Lunch and Dinner 6 days a week, served in our family dining room (we ate with them). Sunday, God rested and so did we!

Every Monday, we would clean their rooms, vacuum, scrub the bathroom, strip the beds, wash the sheets, then remake the beds with the fresh sheets.

To this day, I silently giggle when some are shocked to learn that I can cook and bake like a pro, from scratch. Lol! Mom cooked EVERY meal, 6 days a week. We were expected to help, set and clear dishes and wash by hand. That was our version of "a dishwasher."

It's an incredible amount of work and planning. I have no idea how she did it without going insane. It's why I know how to make pie crusts, breads, soups, stews, roasts etc from scratch. AND I make a mean "Hospital Corner" on the rare occasion I make a bed nowadays.

My husband was understandably impressed when we first dated, as I condescendingly pointed out that his hospital corner was sloppy. Then I ripped apart the bed and showed him how it was done. He just looked at me like—"What The . . .???" Still cracks me up.

Anyway, instead of spending the extra money on little luxuries, which I'm sure was very tempting—they socked away every penny, like little squirrels.

Ultimately, they bought a rental property—and the games began.

The Cliff Notes

Throughout our childhood, my parents would buy, sell and flip—rental properties with an intuitive level of savviness that would shock most. We were always having to go to one property or another to clean or paint them, after renters moved out.

There wasn't a lot of extra money, the rentals were for the future. They'd sell one, then roll the money into a bigger one. Then, they'd sell the "bigger" one, and buy 2 Triplexes. Things like that.

Instead of selling, then pocketing the money—which again, as a military family it would have been nice to have—*they chose* to be disciplined for the long-term goal.

As friends were going off on fancy vacations or buying pricey clothes or random shopping trips throughout the school year—we did not. We took motorhome trips and camped in KOA parks, went to Disneyland in the motorhome one summer, and had the best time. Honestly, those are some of my best, most awesome memories. Kids don't need to take a private plane to Europe to experience the world. I'm just sayin'.

Dad served 25 years in the Coast Guard, retiring at about age 40. He enrolled in the local Community College, to get his high-school GED, so that he could sell Real Estate professionally. He studied, got his GED, then studied for and got his Real Estate license.

There's the 10/90 Rule again. *Instead of* saying "I can't because I don't have a high-school diploma. I had to leave school to pick cotton..." (*10% what happens*), he said, "I'll enroll, study and get my GED. Then, I'll get my Real Estate license" *(90% how you respond).*

He was Rookie of the Year, his first year. I remember him cold-calling from the house, on our *rotary phone*! He had a paper list of names in his hand, and would just hammer out call, after call, after call. In sales we call that "Smiling and Dialing."

Plan the Work then Work the Plan. Today, Livin' the Dream

My parents fully retired when they were about 60, which was 13 years ago. 40 solid years of sacrifice, incredible discipline, hard, hard work and a belief in themselves, paid off big time for them.

They accomplished exactly what they set out to do, as 21-year old newlyweds: Have a happy, healthy family, a happy healthy marriage, and financial security with passive income such that they can fully enjoy their lives together.

My parents bought, flipped and sold their way into owning 2 very large apartment complexes that generate the passive income they sought. As I write this, they just purchased their "forever" dream home. A gorgeous, oceanfront home with 180 degree sweeping views of the Pacific Ocean, on the San Diego coastline.

It is the kind of home you'd see on a magazine cover. It's ½ a mile from my husband and me, and

½ a mile the other way from my sister. Exactly what they wanted. No 2 people, are more deserving.

From picking cotton with an 8th grade education, to this.

I write this not to brag. Braggarts suck. *I want you to be inspired!* My hope, is that you see what they did and think "Ah-ha! I get it . . ." And apply the same principles to your own life, to live exactly the way you want to live.

You CAN do it—the choice is completely yours.

Life is 10% *what happens* to you, 90% *how you handle it.*

Handle it in a way that *serves* your forward momentum. Peace out.

RULE #12
The fine art of not giving a f*ck.

Badass women aren't intimidated by other people's opinions of what they do, or who they are.

She has learned that those who bark the loudest, are the ones who are most intimidated by her strength. She pays them no mind—but if they cross the line, she will artfully put them in their place.

She's usually learned this from being hurt in the past, by those who felt uncomfortable with her sense of self. She's was just being herself. She didn't understand why some took to name-calling and trying to tear her down. Now she understands and it won't happen again.

*She has mastered the fine art of not giving a f*ck.* Crass? Yup. It is also one of the most powerful tools to have in your arsenal. The ability to rise above the negativity of other people's insecurities that manifest themselves in hurtful words, comments or actions is life-changing.

When you are able to truly "get", that the maliciousness is *not* directed at *you*, but at their own discomfort with *themselves,* it's hard to feel hurt.

Let me give you an example:

About a month ago, there was a nice feel-good story on Prince Harry and his new wife Megan Markle. They were attending some sort of a charity event and were shown walking hand-in-hand towards the event. They looked so happy and excited. Pretty benign, but a nice story.

Like a train-wreck, I had to look at some of the comments. Sure enough, there were a handful of mean-spirited comments from other women, tearing her down on everything from her outfit, to her ankles (?), her choice of hairstyle—even saying that she looked "desperate" holding his hand too tight.

Think logically—what feelings do you *really think* are behind the mean-spirited comments? People who are happy and secure, don't vent on others like this. Jealousy, discomfort with themselves and unhappiness or discontent with their own lives, *is amplified* when they see someone else living in a way or doing something that they cannot. It then ignites feelings of anger and resentment which they take out on someone else.

When you are the target of unprovoked malicious words or comments from others, remember this example. Chances are, you are triggering something within the perpetrator that highlights or amplifies feelings of his or her own perceived inadequacies and discontent with life. When you understand this, it's much harder to care or take their comments to heart.

The Chihuahua and the German Shepard. Frightened dogs bark loudest

I thought of the perfect analogy for this Rule, when I was walking my dogs the other day. We were about halfway through the walk, just enjoying the sunshine and fall beach weather, when I heard the frenzied, high-pitched, squealing/yapping of what sounded like a small dog.

I looked to the other side of the street, where the yapping seemed to be originating. There, a tiny little yellow chihuahua was literally *freaking out*, shaking, barking as viciously as he could, trying desperately to lunge at another dog, despite the owner holding him back.

About 6 feet away from him, I saw the issue. Another neighbor was out, casually walking his beautiful, very large German Shepard on the same side of the street. Despite the antics from the other dog, the Shepard was completely calm, cool and relaxed, as he cocked his head to the side and just watched the show.

The Shepard didn't utter a sound. He didn't even flinch a muscle. He just looked at the Chihuahua like "What's your problem?" Then when he's seen enough, casually sauntered away to finish his walk. Chances are, had the Chihuahua kept quiet—the Shepard would've never even noticed him in the first place.

The moral of the story: The Shepard knows his power. That's why he's calm and relaxed. The Chihuahua *also* knows the Shepard's power, that's why he's *not* relaxed.

Frightened dogs bark the loudest. Remember that, next time someone tries to make you feel less than what you are.

Here is the cold hard truth:

- You will never *please* everyone. That is more than ok. Not everyone's opinion matters.
- You will never *be liked* by everyone. Even the most beloved people have haters. Let it go.
- People will say unkind, hurtful things about you. So what—it doesn't change your truth.
- Regardless of the nobility of your cause, *someone* will take issue with it. That's fine. If they don't like it, they don't have to participate.

I've often summed it up this way:

You could cure cancer and save puppies in a single day, and someone, somewhere is going to take issue that you didn't cure diabetes and save cats instead.

Recognize the basic need to be liked

Listen, it's *normal* to want others to like us, agree with our choices, accept us into the group, love our new outfit or hairstyle. Why do you think it feels good to get a ton of "likes" or "followers"? Because in some small way it says, "I like you!"

Have you ever planned to break-up with someone, but they break-up with you *first*? Were you relieved, or did it sort of bother you on some level? Truth—it bugged me. I wanted to be the one doing the breaking-up! I had the whole "it's not you, it's me" speech ready, complete with compliments and assurances that he would make someone very happy.

Before I could do it, *he* initiates the break-up AND uses my "it's not you, it's me" speech. I was so bugged! Not because I liked him or wanted to be with him. I didn't. When I dug deep, it was because truthfully, *I felt slightly hurt that I was rejected.* The "who" didn't matter. It was the rejection of another human being.

The same principle can be used for unkind comments online or from people around you. Chances are, you've had a few trolls on your social media pages over the years. Think about how you felt when you read mean comments. It probably hurt a little, then turned into mild anger.

But why? Did the comment really alter your life in anyway? Did your family stop loving you? Did it take away your life's accomplishments, or diminish your value as a person? No. It only poked at the ego, and the need to feel liked. Nothing more. Recognize it. Now let it go.

At a fundamental level we *all* want to feel liked, loved and accepted for who we truly are, faults and all. Think about the people in your life, who fit the bill. These are "your people." They're probably family, spouse, and a handful of true friends.

The reality is that there are a lot of hurting people in the world, needlessly venting their insecurities, unhappiness, jealousy or frustration with life out on others. You've probably experienced this. I know I have. That is why I say . . .

Not everyone's opinion matters

This mantra is a powerful way to filter out the noise and distraction that comes from putting too much stock into caring what the *wrong* people think. Understanding whose opinion matters and whose does not, has the power to change your life because it provides focus.

Badass women are able to separate those who give *constructive criticism* meant to create positive growth in her, from the insecure people throwing *destructive criticism* meant to belittle or knock her down. That is the meaning of "not everyone's opinion matters."

A true badass, is woman enough to face her own shortcomings because she wants to get better. Therefore, she welcomes *constructive* criticism or feedback from those she loves, trusts and respects. She knows they have her best interests in mind. *Constructive criticism facilitates our growth and evolution.*

For example, if I give a public speech, and afterwards my mom says overall it was good, but there were a couple areas that didn't translate well—I'm going to listen to her. I know she has my best interests at heart, wanting only the best for me. I am going to take what she said into consideration. Ultimately I'll make my own decision, but I listen and accept the feedback.

If, during an annual Job Performance review, my boss identifies areas of improvement for me to focus, I'm going to listen. That being said, my last boss was my biggest fan and always supported initiatives I put forth. I knew he had my best interests at heart, so his feedback held a lot of weight. If he's identifying areas for me to focus, I'm going to do it. That is constructive feedback. Make sense?

Opinions that do *not matter,* are from those passing judgement from a place rooted in hatred, jealousy, insecurity, or resentment. These can be online-trolls, strangers, co-workers, "friends", acquaintances, even some family members. I promise, you know the people in your life who belong in this category. *This* is where you practice the fine art of not giving a f*ck!

Don't ever listen to what anyone says! #Eyeroll

I seriously eyeroll when I hear someone say "Don't ever listen to what anyone else says! " That's just asinine. You can't go through life, literally ignoring *everything everyone* says, if it's contrary to your own opinion or desire.

That is not how you grow and get better. Positive growth comes from a very unique balance of confidence and belief-in-self, *along with* the ability to intuitively separate feedback that is constructive and well-intentioned, from that which is meant to belittle and hurt.

It comes from listening with an open mind, to those you love and trust, but in the end making up your own mind, following your own path. Those that love us, have the best of intentions—but only *you* know what is best for you.

RULE #13
Life's BIGGEST mistakes are made when we ignore our intuition

The biggest mistakes in life are made when you let your HEAD talk you out of what you GUT, or intuition is telling you.

Women have a much higher level of intuitive awareness. We *know* when something or someone isn't right. We *know* when to steer clear. Men have physical strength as their form of self-protection. Intuition, *is our* form of self-protection—and that is much more powerful than physical strength. The key is to understand your power and embrace, not dismiss it.

How many times have you said, "I KNEW it!!" to something or someone, that initially gave you a bad feeling, but you did it anyway because it made sense, intellectually?

We are given the gift of intuition for a reason. It guides us away from certain situations, or people who may bring us harm. It whispers to us, when we ask for guidance or direction during difficult times or decisions. We either listen, or intellectually justify our way into an alternate route.

Have you ever had a weird feeling that something wasn't right with your significant other? You couldn't put your finger on it, but something definitely felt off. I'll bet that 10 out of 10 times, you were absolutely right. However, if you let your head overrule your intuition by saying, "Oh I'm just being overly sensitive, I'm sure everything's fine", chances are you kicked yourself later and said "I knew it." This is what I'm talking about.

Honor your intuition. It is your secret-weapon-super-power.

We've been discouraged from using this power

Our entire culture is rooted in patriarchy and the inflated value of traditional male qualities over traditional female qualities, which have been incorrectly ridiculed as inferior.

Even the way in which we define things, is very male-based. The male mentality of "someone has to lose, so that I can win," permeates our culture. When we refer to someone as successful, it usually means they hold some sort of prestigious position, with a respectable net worth. He who has the most toys, wins. That is a male-based way of thought.

Built by men, Corporate America was set-up to thrive on and value male-based ways of thought, communication and structure. In order to succeed within the structure, we as women have had to learn to adapt to their rules. It is like learning to write with your left hand, when you're right-handed. It's awkward at times, but we do it. In heels.

For example, in business, the expectation is to back decisions and arguments solely with stats, data, logic and objective facts. Part of this is good and does add value in decision making. However, I propose that basing decisions solely on male-based thought, is just as ineffective as basing them solely on a female way of thought.

Using intuition only

Can you even *imagine* the eye-rolling, if in a meeting you said, "I know the data points Left, but I have a *feeling* we should go Right..." I hate to say it, but your male colleagues won't be impressed.

As women, we intuitively know not to go down the rabbit hole of saying, "I just have a feeling." As a result, we subconsciously adopt the male-based way of thought, and present positions based upon what the facts support—and many times leave our intuition out of it.

Use it or lose it

What happens when you don't exercise a part of your body? It atrophies. It becomes weaker. It is the same with our intuitive powers. If we constantly allow our head to override our intuition—it becomes increasingly more difficult for us to tap into it. Don't let that happen. It is a powerful internal compass. Listen to it, use it.

For clarity, I am not advocating flying through life on intuition alone. Rather, let's understand the value of *integrating both* male and female ways of thought, to achieve the greatest value.

When intuition is extremely strong, and in direct opposition to the facts

There are those times when despite the presence of overwhelming, objective facts, evidence and data clearly pointing one way, our intuition desperately screams at us "NO! DO NOT ENTER! DO NOT DO IT!" If you're smart, you'll honor the intuition and be glad you did.

When the intuition is strong, and in direct opposition to objective facts—intuition always wins. I know this now, but I had to learn it the hard way. Here's my story . . .

Keepin' It Real . . .

I was a Regional VP for a telecom company, responsible for multiple sales offices throughout SoCal (Southern California) and Vegas. Each office was headed by a Sales Manager who led teams of 10-12 salespeople and support staff. The Sales Managers then reported up to me.

Over the course of 6-months, a Sales Manager for one of our competitors (let's call him "Vinny") had been hammering me via phone, for an interview. He had heard that my LA Manager was on the chopping block, and he wanted to be considered for the position.

Technically, Vinny did everything right. A sales manager (or sales person) *should* exhibit a level of courteous persistence, timely follow-up, and articulately outline why he/she should be considered—which he did.

On paper, Vinny's resume was rock-solid. I checked around, and by all accounts, his numbers were strong. There was no viable, objective basis to deny him an interview, *except intuitively, I couldn't stand him.*

I felt guilty for stereotyping him

I know this is going to sound mean, but I'm going to be 100% honest. At the time, I attributed my disdain for him, because he struck me as the stereotypical brash, fast-talking, Jersey-Shore, macho-sexist-Italian guy. I envisioned a gold-nugget necklace, greased back hair, doused in Drakaar Noir, tapping me on the butt and telling me to get him a cup of Kwoff-ee, sweetie. I knew it was unfair of me.

Ultimately, I did agree to grant him an in-person interview. After 6-months, we would finally meet in person. The day comes, he arrives, and I walk out to meet VINNY. Straight out of Central Casting: Super tan, extra white capped teeth, black greased back hair, semi-shiny suit (impeccable of course), big gold watch *and a gold nugget necklace!!! LOL.* He was probably 10-years older than I was at the time and looked exactly as I had pictured. I was waiting for the fist-pumping.

He interviewed *perfectly.* Technically, Vinny was flawless. He was appropriately deferent, answered every question thoroughly, presented proof of performance—everything. Plus, he indicated that he had several very large deals in the pipeline, that he would bring over to the LA office, if hired. Pretty tempting.

After the interview, instead of feeling better about him, I felt worse. I just had a *bad, bad* feeling about the guy. *That's when my head took over, overriding my intuition, with the objective facts.*

It's not you, it's ME

Ultimately, I talked myself into believing that it wasn't *him*, it was *me*. I was allowing my own aversion to "that type of a guy", to override a good candidate. Worse yet, I felt *awful* and *guilty* for denying him a job, based off of what I thought were my own prejudices and stereotypes. I knew firsthand how it felt to be judged and categorized, and I felt ashamed for doing the same thing to someone else.

Against my intuition, but in alignment with the data, I hired him.

As promised, Vinny brought over the business he promised. For the next 6 months, he blew out the LA team's sales numbers, sending me large contracts to sign/approve. I looked them over carefully—they were legit. Wow! Glad I put my feelings aside and made a smart-hire based on the facts!

It's all fun and games till someone skips town and goes on the lamb . . .

I was in the LA office one morning, (from my home base in San Diego), using Vinny's office to take calls. It was pretty early, and I wasn't expecting him in for another hour or so.

What happened next, still seems like a slo-mo dream. The door opens, and in walks our HR Director *and* the HR SVP (Senior Vice President). Our corporate offices were based in Northern California, which meant that they had flown-in on the first available flight *and* hadn't notified me. Crap.

I had always been super friendly with both and considered them work-friends. The look on their faces clearly indicated that this was not a social visit.

My blood ran cold. "Crap. This can't be good", I thought. They closed the door, briefcases and files in hand, asking for Vinny. I advised that he wasn't due for another hour at which point the SVP said "That's fine. We need to talk to you first, Shelli." Omg.

For the next 2 hours, which felt like 2 days—I was cross-examined and grilled on every crevice of my relationship with Vinny. How did you know him, what is the nature of your relationship, did you know him prior to employment, why did you hire him over other candidates, how was he able to close large deals so quickly,—on and on.

They refused to disclose the purpose of their line of questioning, until the very end, when it was clear that I didn't have knowledge of his shenanigans.

In short, he had been submitting falsified orders for non-existent companies, at non-existent OR vacant addresses throughout California. As was typical at the time, telecom companies would pay commissions on submitted orders at the end of each month, yet it would take 6-8 months for the actual service to be provisioned. In other words, he had 6-8 months before you-know-what hit the fan.

In the meantime, he totally worked the Compensation Plan. He'd structure his monthly orders to max-out the accelerators (the more you sell, the higher your percentage of the sale). At that time, using Google to verify an address or company wasn't as typical, plus in all honestly, the checks and balances in telecom ran pretty loose. That is in part, why the tech bubble burst.

I sat, frozen. We waited for Vinny to arrive at the office. And waited. And waited. Numerous calls went to voicemail. He must have been tipped off that HR was in the office, put 2 and 2 together, and no joke, *skipped town*. Never heard from him again, to my knowledge.

I was kicking myself!!! I knew something wasn't right with him and I talked myself out of it.

Here were the consequences, of ignoring my intuition:

- The company conducted a full investigation on me, to ensure I wasn't involved.
- I was *extremely* close to getting fired. It was only because I was considered "highly-valued" *and* his scam was so intricate, that they couldn't ding me for negligence.

- The event tarnished my reputation, sullied the entire Region, and all but ensured I was no longer considered promotable within the organization.
- The reputation I had built for strong judgment and good hires, was diminished.

You can bet that now, I listen to my gut with full radar ears. The awesome thing is, the more I listen and honor my intuition—the stronger and louder it gets. That's because it is being exercised—just like working out. The more consistent you are, the stronger it gets.

RULE #14
Live the life that makes YOU happy.

From time to time, I'll accompany Oliver to a professional event or dinner, where I really don't know anyone. Within minutes I'm happily gabbing away, listening to people's stories, asking them questions, and learning interesting tidbits about their lives and way of thinking.

Without exception, my more reserved husband, has to pry me away from the event, often saying "What in the heck did you find to talk about with so-and-so? I never know what to say past "Hi, how's business?" "I dunno", I'll say, "I asked him if he'd choose his line of work all over again, if given the chance...and it was really interesting what he said..."

Life works, because we are all different. We are all unique, with our own set of values, desires, interests, likes, dislikes, dreams and **happy-levers**: *Things that flat out, bring us genuine, authentic happiness at a base level.*

In short, the Life-Path that bring *me* true happiness— isn't necessarily the same one that would bring *you* true happiness. That is more than ok, it is how we are built.

Discontent, unhappiness and frustration in life, at varying levels, take root when you allow yourself to be sucked into the vortex of a life-path that may make *others* happy—but *doesn't make YOU happy.*

Discontent is further amplified, when we reject the option to *change paths*, and instead—stay on the less authentic road due to obligations or the expectations of others.

Getting sucked into the vortex

More often than not, we are pulled into the vortex of pursuing a particular career or living a certain type of life, because it's what we are supposed to do, or it would make the parents proud / happy, or we somehow feel obligated.

If you are in the enviable position of just starting out in life, I would encourage you to choose the path MOST in alignment with your natural gifts and aptitudes. These are the things that make you feel most at peace & grounded.

Certain things come to us more naturally than other things.

For example, leadership comes to me more naturally, than Math & Accounting.

Let's say I muscle my way through CPA school.

- I end up with a nice lifestyle.
- My parents are proud of me.
- It sounds good at a cocktail party.

But, what is the personal price I pay? The personal price is high. Every single day, I cannot escape the feeling that my life has amounted to shoving the metaphoric square peg through a round hole and acting happy about it.

I am **out of alignment**. I am constantly **swimming upstream**—and it is exhausting. Sounds pretty fricking miserable, Right!?

If something comes to you easily—it is because you are supposed to do something with it. Don't block it out. Embrace it into your life!!

Like the make-up lady at Nordstrom said, when I asked if the neon pink lipstick looked good on me... (shrug) "You do YOU, Boo."

If you think you've made a mistake or have outgrown and evolved beyond your current path—CHANGE COURSE. Yes—you really, really can.

Following someone else's dream

I'm going to go out on a limb and say that the idea of taking a particular life-path for reasons *other than* it is your true heart's desire, rings true for most everyone.

Whether that manifested itself in the form of your choice of education, career, choice of spouse, lifestyle, where you live, kids or no kids—I think most every person has traveled, if even briefly—a lifepath based on a conscious or subconscious self-imposed obligation. That is, taking the expected path, what society deems acceptable or what would make others (usually parents and family) . . . proud of them.

It's a strong human desire. The need to feel accepted and respected by others, the desire to feel our parents pride in our accomplishments, are extremely strong, intoxicating emotions. To a large extent, they play a key role in *why* we choose the path in the first place, but moreover . . . why we ***stay*** *on* a lifepath that isn't our calling.

At the time, I really DID want that . . . now it has changed

I would agree that this statement, is probably very true, for non-major life decisions. After all, as you grow, mature and evolve—what you really *did* want at 20, isn't necessarily what you want at 40. At 20, maybe it *was* super cool to live downtown in a high-rise apartment. At 40, taking the elevator up and down 30 floors so the dog can pee 4x a day, sounds like a pain in the rear.

What you look for in a guy at 25, is probably pretty different than what you'd look for at 35. At 25, my requirements were: Must be hot. Must have job. The list got a little more comprehensive a few years later. I'm just sayin' . . . .

As we grow and evolve, we understand more about life and what is important. Therefore, what we want changes as well.

I am referring moreover, to the big life decisions we make out of obligation, a desire to feel accepted or a feeling that it is the natural next step. Sometimes we convince ourselves that it's what we want, because we believe it will make life easier rather than to rock the boat.

Some examples:

1. You come from a family of physicians, and it is expected that you will carry on the family tradition, even though your true love is music. Dutifully, you enter medical school, go through the motions, and pursue a career as a physician.

2. You've always wanted to become a Newscaster and travel the world. You've also been dating a great guy for the past 5 years. The chatter from parents, friends and family, to get married and start a family has become incessant. He proposes, you get married and start a family, never pursuing your dream.

Many have experienced following a particular Life-Path out obligation OR living a Life-Path we talked ourselves into at some point, but now realize, it isn't our true calling.

I've walked this same road

I've walked this exact road, taking the path I felt was naturally expected of me, and the one that would make my parents proud. Then one day, like a racehorse stuck in a locked stable—I kicked the stable door as hard as I could and bolted for open field. *Here's my story . . .*

Keepin' It Real . . .

The most important, life-altering, Maverick-Moment of my life

I started dating James when we were both 17-year old high-school Juniors in Seattle. We attended a private, Catholic, college-prep high-school. Me, on financial aid, he—from a wealthy Seattle family.

We had 1st period Study Hall together, which for me meant a *full hour of power . . .* socializing! For him, it meant . . . *studying*? What was THAT about?

Every morning, he would walk into Study Hall with the Wall Street Journal, multiple textbooks and thermos of coffee to sip as he read the financials in the Journal . . . Yes, I'm totally serious. He was an old soul. I seriously think he popped out of the womb, a 50-year old lawyer . . . .which ironically, is what he became—a lawyer. Distinguished, I'm sure.

He was a jock star, in both wresting and football. He was oddly brilliant, interesting, stoic, somewhat introverted, philosophical and driven. I was an athlete, having studied ballet since age 3.

I was a super social extrovert, bubbly, had lots of friends, went to all the games and parties, and never at a loss for dates. It was a good time.

I thought he was cute of course, plus I liked athletes. Tee he he! He'd always sit across from me, listening as I went on and on about god knows what. I remember him looking at me like I was some sort of an interesting specimen. He asked me to the Christmas Ball, and the rest is history.

My parents loved him, his parents loved me—it was a solid situation. We would date for the next 9 years, except for a few "breaks", always initiated by me... that probably should have been my first clue.

He treated me like a princess. Our 1st Valentine's Day, I remember him jogging down the walkway to our backdoor, with roses, a card and a big box of my favorite Sees Chocolates in hand.

"I only got you a card?" I said. To which he responded, "The guy buys gifts for the girl. Not the other way around." Whoa! I can live with that!

He was very traditional, which at that age, in the bubble of high-school and living at home, only manifested itself in the form of what I knew to be gentlemanly behavior. Things like opening doors, picking me up, asking for dates well in advance, having me home by curfew, being respectful to my parents, etc.

With my dad, who was born and raised in the deep South, and served 25 years in the Coast Guard—I was accustomed to gentlemanly manners. To this day, Dad *still* opens my mom's doors, seats her first in the car, and when she calls his name—endearingly responds "Ma'am?" So that was what I saw, and what I expected without *knowing* I expected it.

We never took turns driving—he always drove. He never allowed me to pick up the tab or pay ½ (mind you, we were in high school). He always took care of everything. When we went to House of Pizza (our favorite!), he always cut a slice and served me first. He was a keeper!

We got engaged at 23, moved to San Diego for him to begin law school, while I transferred to the USD undergrad program. We married the following summer in a large, lavish, all-the-bells-and-whistles wedding at his parents Country Club. And yes—I had a huge white dress with puffy shoulders and a 20 mile train. At the end of summer, we went back to San Diego and resumed school, as a newly married couple.

It's funny how exponential our growth and evolution is from teenage years, to young adulthood. Once out from under your parents, and the bubble of high-school, your core characteristics, basic beliefs and view of the world, blossom and evolve.

It's the natural progression of finding your own way in the world. Especially with relationships that start very young and continue into adulthood. You either grow together or realize that you want very different things.

If you end up wanting very different things out of life, you've got a decision:

1. STAY, knowing there will always be an element of tension in the relationship, because one person is bound to feel that he/she sacrificed more.

2 GO, understanding that the relationship ran its course, and both deserve to pursue the life they want to live.

In one moment in time, I realized that we wanted very different things. I remember the moment so clearly, it may as well have happened yesterday.

The watershed moment—it all came down to one brief conversation:

We were on campus, sitting in his black convertible Toyota, talking about school. I was 2 quarters away from a degree in Media Communications and was talking excitedly about ruling the world as a journalist and News Anchor. I had interned at the ABC affiliate in Seattle, and caught the bug!

I noticed that he was staring straight ahead, and once I stopped talking—complete silence. Hello?? He turned to me, confusion wafting across his face, as though seeing me for the very first time in his life.

The conversation that ended it all, went like this:

Him: "Well... you'll do *something* to keep yourself busy, but we're going to start having kids—and then you'll be at home.

Me: Stunned. My brain froze, time stood still. What is he talking about??
Finally, I choked out "No I'm not? Why do I have to give up my dreams just because I'm the woman?"

Him: "But what kind of a mother would you be, working and not home with them?"

Me: "Same kind of father you would be, working and not home with them. Why don't YOU stay home?"

Him: "Because I'm going to be a lawyer."

Me: "Well I'm going to be a News Anchor."

That was the turning point. Very shortly thereafter, I made the announcement that I wanted out—and all hell broke loose.

Both sets of parents were in a complete tizzy. I was the complete evil perpetrator among all of our friends from high-school, my parents were SO upset and angry with me, believing I was making a HUGE mistake.

Honestly, I don't blame my parents a bit. I would have felt the same way, if it was my daughter. For them, their strong-willed daughter had decided 1-year into the marriage, of a 9-year relationship—that she "was done" and wasn't going to listen to anyone. It had to have been so frustrating and traumatizing for them.

James packed up and transferred to the University of Washington Law School, where he finished. My parents made me come back home, to go to Marriage Counseling, which I did. Once.

We were sitting in the poor counselor's office, my arms folded like a petulant child being made to talk to her, and all I remember saying is this . . . *"I feel like an ant, laying on my back with a straight-pin stuck through my stomach, pinning me to the ground. I can wiggle my arms and legs, but I can't move, and I can't go anywhere . . ."*

I could tell by the look on her face, and silence—she knew I was done. I didn't go back, and I stuck to my guns.

I left the marriage with a couple dollars to my name, took the bus downtown to the biggest employment agency in Seattle, and within a few weeks accepted a job-offer as an entry-level Sales Executive for a Telecomm company.

I flew to the 1-week mandatory Sales Training course where they sent all new-hire Rookies. It was a week of luxury at the Embassy Suites in San Jose. It was 7am—7pm sales training, with intensive, inevitably humiliating Sales Role-Playing.

Humiliating, because we were all just out of college, learning how to sell. The group leaders would act as the "Prospective Client" and each new-hire had to play the role of "salesperson" in front of our group of 25.

Of course the goal is to make the sale as hard as possible to challenge us, so the "Client" was always extra cantankerous, argumentative and wouldn't stipulate to anything you said. Which of course means, you're bound to look like a complete fool. Which I did, many, many times!

After sales training, I worked as hard as possible. I stayed in the field cold-calling businesses every day until it was dark. After a few months, I had ranked as the Seattle office's top sales performer for 3 consecutive months, and 2nd in the Western Region. As promised, the Sales Manager approved my transfer to the San Diego office.

No regrets

I transferred to San Diego, and never looked back at my old life with James. Not even once.

I have never, never, ever—regretted my decision. I knew with every fiber of my being, that I didn't want to live a life less than what I had envisioned. Not too far beneath the surface, I had an impenetrable knowledge that if I stayed, I would suffocate.

I found it in me to barrel straight through the drama, regardless of the resistance, warning and disapproval I got from pretty much everyone around me. I knew that staying, would have made my life much easier in the *short-term*.

He would have continued to take care of me, money would have never been an issue, I'd live in a beautiful home, with a successful husband and a cozy life. I knew that. But the price was far, far too dear. I didn't want a cozy, safe life—I wanted to blaze my own trail and take a big bite of the apple for myself.

I did not want to walk the life-path of playing "Vice President" to his "President." That was his view of the gender roles. I would always play a supporting role, based solely on my gender, not my goals, dreams and drive . . . and that wasn't ok with me.

I remember "seeing myself" 20 years down the road, with a life that most would give their right arm for . . . But feeling discontent, knowing I took the safe road and not the one *that I personally* wanted for myself. I saw myself depressed at squandering talents, not taking chances—not seeing what I *could have* done.

The point is, each person should be free to follow the path that authentically resonates with them . . . In my case, it was the unpopular road. For others, it may truly be the popular road. Either way—let each human being choose their own, authentic path without judgement, marginalization or criticism. We will all be better for it.

From lawyer to yoga instructor . . .

This is a true story, that I came across during Yoga class last week. Coincidentally (is anything really just coincidence?) it was perfect timing as I was about to write this section about daring to follow your own true path!

As many of you may know, from reading my last book, *Toxic Pebbles—Transform Your Life*, I am a huge advocate of taking care of yourself, both inside and out. I counter my 5x a week Boot-Camp routine, with my favorite Hot Yoga class. It helps to center, ground and calm me from the week.

I've been taking class from this particular Instructor for at least 2-years. I'm guessing she's in her late 20's, maybe 30. She lights up the room with her smile and energy, always beginning class with a thoughtful, introspective perspective about life and living in the moment.

If ever I've seen someone who really, really loves what she does—it is her! I really didn't think much about her background, assuming that she probably graduated from college, then went into Yoga practice. That wasn't the case.

It was during the last class, that we all learned something interesting. She shared that she had graduated law school, passed the Bar, and started her career as an attorney.

It wasn't for me

It wasn't long before she realized this was not her path. It was going through the motions, doing what was expected, but feeling like a square peg in a round hold.

Abruptly, she changed paths, left the legal field, enrolled in Teacher Training and became a certified Yoga instructor. Today, she is happily doing what she loves to do. It makes sense now. Always, without exception—she seems so calm, authentically happy and grateful to be there.

I could only imagine the major eyebrow raises and undoubtedly, the push-back she received from friends and family over such a major decision. I know how expensive law school is. Whether her family paid for her education, or it was through student loans—the fact of the matter is, it is very, very expensive.

For her, it probably took going down the path-of-expectations for a few years, to truly appreciate the opportunity to do what you truly love.

Be that as it may, what she did takes some serious chutzpah, a spine of steel and an undeniable belief in self. To have that at such a young age . . . She will do just fine.

RULE #15

The 5 people you spend the most time with, either add to detract from your life course. Choose mindfully and wisely.

"You are the average of the five people you spend the most time with."—Jim Rohn

Think about that . . . if this is true, then the people with whom you choose to spend the most time, *influences* the person you eventually become. They affect your thoughts and actions, they can work to either *elevate* your life or *bring your life down*.

Many times we make friends *mindlessly*, spending time with them simply because it's convenient. Maybe you work together, or live close by, or they're part of "the group" so it's easy.

When you begin to think more critically in terms of the influence they have on your life, ask yourself:

- Who are your 5 people?
- Would you choose the same 5?
- Why or why not?

- Who would you keep?
- Who would you eliminate?
- Are they positive, enlightening and inspirational, or negative, bitter and unhappy?
- What does each person add to your life?

You could be the strongest, happiest, most confident, positive person on the face of the earth, but if you constantly surround yourself with negative, fear-based people, it *will* affect your life's progression.

If you are exceptionally strong and grounded, the impact will be much smaller, but you lose out on the *positive benefits* you would have absorbed from a more elevated group.

Instead, mindfully seek out people you admire, who inspire you to think bigger, to be a better person, to grow and evolve in positivity and light. Surround yourself with people who have an exciting, positive mindset and see life and the glass as half full—not half empty.

Being around these types of people will naturally *raise* your vibration to meet theirs. In turn, the Universe will respond by bringing more positive things into your life. Negative thoughts and energy attracts more of the same. Positive thoughts and energy, attracts more of the same.

RULE #16
Understand that you *always* have the power of choice. Always.

Understanding that the power of choice is *always* in your hands, is one of the most empowering, liberating, confidence-building Badass Rules there are. When feeling frustrated, overwhelmed, stressed or trapped—knowing that *you can* opt out, is psychologically powerful.

Though you may decide *not* to opt out after weighing the consequences—the knowledge that you *can*, if you really, really want to, is key to getting through whatever it is that is weighing you down.

The power to choose applies to virtually every area of life, from the infinitesimal to huge life-changing decisions. Many find this concept difficult to grasp, immediately citing a slew of examples in their own lives where they claim not to have a choice.

Common example, "I can't leave my professional field. I don't have a choice—it pays well, and we've got a big mortgage, high car-payments, kids in private schools."

The truth of the matter is, this person *can* choose to leave her professional field. *The question, is whether or not she is willing to accept the consequences of the decision—right?*

If she really wanted out, she could sell the big home and buy something less expensive, trade-in the pricey cars for more moderate options, put the kids in public schools, and downsize her lifestyle overall, in order to accommodate a career change.

The power to choose is there. The real question is, "Is the juice worth the squeeze?" If not, she stays. If so, she makes the needed changes.

People will usually say *"I can't"* not because they truly cannot, but for one of 3 reasons:

- The consequences are too high.
- It isn't important enough. Not a priority.
- It's too much hassle. Don't really want to do it.

Let's look at 3 examples:

1. **I can't work-out because I have to get kids to school and be to work by 9am.**

   I hear this a lot, and yes I get it. Without a doubt, that is a full-schedule, requiring more effort and planning in comparison to other people's situations. In reality, there are a variety of solutions, including:

A. Workout in the AM. Get up an hour before the kids, pop in a DVD or Stream a favorite workout from the comfort of home. Set out mat, weights, water and workout clothes the night before.

B. Workout during lunch hour. Keep freshen-up toiletries in a small cosmetic bag at work.

C. Workout after work. Go to the gym on the way home, OR workout from home via DVD or streaming.

When someone is quick with excuses for any proposed solution, chances are, it just isn't important enough to them, or they really don't want to do it. There is nothing wrong with that. But just be honest and say, "I *can* but I don't want to put forth the effort, at least right now."

It generates more personal power to say *I can, but choose not to*—vs imposing false limitations on yourself with the words, "*I can't.*"

2. I can't quit my job / change professions because I have a mortgage, car payment, bills, etc . . .

Remember years ago, the male Flight Attendant who on a particular flight, told a bitchy passenger to "F-off", popped open a can of beer, and slid down the plane's inflatable evacuation slide to freedom (and no job)? I laughed so hard when I heard that, I could barely breathe. It was all over TV, with people cheering him on in recognition of his feelings—and living somewhat vicariously.

Who *hasn't* felt like jumping down the metaphoric inflatable slide, cocktail in hand? You know, those times when you've really just "had it up to here" with it all. The stress, cranky customers, endless bills, the drama, and the never-ending treadmill called life, can take its mental, physical and emotional toll on a person.

That was funny to see on TV, but I can't wait to tell you this real-life story that I encountered, when interviewing attorneys for my husband's Firm.

Ummm, I just want to sell snow cones

Oliver's (my husband) law firm, had a job opening for another attorney. Because of my background, I agreed to vet resumes and conduct phone-interviews with qualified candidates, sending the top 3 to the firm for in-person interviews.

One candidate had a near perfect resume on paper. He had been a Partner with another firm for over 20 years, in the same field as Oliver's firm. That would translate to a quick ramp-up time, plus nuanced knowledge of the industry and its players.

He did have a 5-year gap in employment, which of course I asked him about during the phone interview. The story he shared, made me smile.

He explained that he had spent 20 years of his life, working 12-hour days, many weekends, dealing with cantankerous lawyers, clients and the volatility of the industry. He and his wife had 2 kids, a large home in a prestigious area of San Diego, complete with Country Club membership, luxury cars, private schools and yearly vacations someplace warm and fancy.

Connecting the dots, I sensed that he made a nice living, but was pretty leveraged. It was a façade. It looked one way on the outside, but under the hood—it was a scramble every month, to cover the lifestyle.

One day, he said that he woke up and decided, *I'm over it*! After taking a little time to figure out logistics and wrap up loose ends . . .

They sold the house and cars. Cancelled club memberships, wrapped up the kid's school—and relocated to one of the Hawaiian Islands *where he opened a snow cone stand by the beach*!

He purchased a few more stands, hired people to run them and enjoyed his own little snow cone business around the island. They rented a small place, had 1 car because they could bike most everywhere, and just lived a simple, streamlined life.

True story! For him—the juice was worth the squeeze.

Most people would have said "I can't because . . . I have a 20-year law practice, kids, a mortgage, bills, cars, etc . . ." This guy decided that he really wanted out. He decided that choosing to forego the lifestyle, house, cars, and memberships was worth it, in exchange for a simpler, more streamlined life.

It ended up being a 5-year sabbatical for him, at which point he was ready to re-enter the legal field. I love this story. I found myself smiling, while listening to him.

The next time you feel stuck in a job, relationship, marriage, or any life situation, look at it from a different perspective. Think about ways you *can* even if it sounds really drastic, undoable—and scares the crap out of you.

Thinking about it, doesn't mean to HAVE to do it. Thinking is free, non-committal, and no knows you're doing it! Think about the Snowcone story for a little inspiration.

I can't call off the wedding—it's too late

True story. A good friend of mine was engaged to be married. Her entire extended family had flown-in from across the country and were all enjoying a mini-reunion at the resort where everyone was staying for the wedding.

I had been with my friend the day before, a few hours before the rehearsal dinner. I could tell something was wrong, so we sat down. She couldn't shake the feeling that she was making a big mistake. Not because he was a bad guy—he was actually just the opposite. Super kind, generous, successful and loved her. For various reasons, she just felt that he wasn't the one.

I knew not to tell her that it was just cold feet. Instead, I said "You're the only one who really knows what's best for you. But I am your friend, and I will support whatever you decide."

The next morning, my boyfriend and I hurried to get ready and out the door for her 9am wedding. Arriving at the church, we milled around outside with other guests, waiting to be seated. It was another gorgeous San Diego day, and I was thinking how pretty the outdoor reception was going to be.

8:55am—I looked around, thinking that they should really be seating people by now. I asked a guy dressed like an usher, if we should sit down. Blank stare. "Oh—Uhh, didn't you hear? She called off the wedding *this morning*."

Omg, she did it, I thought. Hoooo-lyyy crap.

Since everything was paid for, they moved forward with the Reception, re-labeling it a "Luncheon" for all of the guests and family from out of town. The now ex-groom could not have been more gracious or exhibited more class. Welcoming everyone at the entrance, he stood in front of the luncheon with a microphone, graciously thanking everyone for coming.

Even more noteworthy, he said "Please, don't be upset with (the bride). I know this isn't the day we all intended, but she did what she felt in her heart was best, and I support her. This is just as difficult for her, so please make her feel welcomed when she arrives." Talk about character and grace under fire. A true class act.

I will also never forget the number of women who secretly came up to my friend at the luncheon, and said "I wish I had the guts to do what you did . . ." Wow!! That blew me away.

I'm talking 4-5 older or middle-aged women, essentially saying that if they had the courage at the time, they would not be married to their husbands! I felt from many, a secret "Atta girl" to her, for having that level of courage, despite the anticipated consequences.

I don't want to give away her identity, but suffice it to say, she did go on to live happily ever after, and quite well, I might add.

The power of choice—it's always yours!

One *BADASS* Career

> Note to Self:
> If you were able to believe in Santa for 8 years,
> you can believe in yourself for 5 seconds.
> You got this!

> # RULE #17
> ### 80% of getting the job, is just *not being* an idiot.

I'm being serious. You would be *shocked* at the number of people who lose out on a job, a promotion, or get themselves fired *not* because they are less qualified, less talented or not as smart as their successors, but because they make idiotic mistakes that get them eliminated before they're even considered.

Badass women are different. They know how to compete and they know how get what they want.

They understand how not to screw up an opportunity, with unforced errors. An *unforced error* is a missed opportunity that is completely the result of your own blunder, and not because someone else was better or more qualified. In short, it's shooting yourself in the foot with a dumb mistake.

As a former executive, I've probably interviewed close to 1,000 job candidates, and ultimately hired over 200-300 from those interviews. I can't even begin to tell you how many resumes I've reviewed before deciding who to call. Probably thousands over the years.

What I *can* tell you, is the alarming number of people who needlessly lost the opportunity over something completely within their control. Sloppy resumes, inappropriate voicemail greetings, poor phone etiquette, careless emails, poor interview judgement—resulted in elimination from job consideration.

These are easy mistakes that I want you to avoid! Don't blow an opportunity over something you can easily control.

Top unforced errors by job candidates. Be aware of these!

1. *Sloppy Resume:* Misspelled words, poor grammar, text out of alignment (they didn't save the doc as a PDF). Spell and grammar check, always.

2. *Unprofessional email address.* If your email address is something like YoBitchezz@gmail, please . . . don't use it to correspond with potential employers. Even if you think it's funny. *Set up a separate, professional email for job seeking.* Keep it neutral.

3. *Poor email etiquette.* If I liked a resume, I emailed the person to request a phone interview. I specifically did this to gauge their level of professionalism in written correspondence. Responding "Hey Shelli", is a no. It's way too informal at this stage.

Err on the side of formality, responding with "Dear (or Good Morning/Afternoon) Ms. Pelly." Remember to always spell and grammar check. Obvious errors communicate a lack of detail or care that most employers will notice.

4. *Inappropriate voicemail greeting.* If you are job-seeking and expecting calls from potential employers, make *sure* that your voicemail greeting is simple, friendly and professional. Meowing and pretending it's your cat on the voicemail greeting is funny to your friends, weird to an employer. Keep everything neutral while interviewing.

5. *Poor phone skills.* If you are job seeking and a call comes through—*assume it is an employer.* Do NOT answer "yeah," "yo" or even "hello?" *Especially* if the call is coming through at the exact time you have a phone interview scheduled!

    I've called people for a scheduled phone-screen, and they literally sounded like they were still in bed answering with a groggy . . . "Yeah?" **Here's how to answer:** Upbeat and friendly, "Good morning this is Shelli." Trust me—you *will* stand out in a good way.

6. *Mucking up the Interview:* By the time someone had an in-person interview with me, they were probably 80% of the way to a job offer. Notwithstanding their skills, here are a few unforced errors that cost candidates the job:

Sloppy dressing or poor grooming. An employer will view you through the eyes of "would he/she make a good impression on our clients OR reflect well on the company." Always err on the side of dressing more formally than not. Clothes should always professional, clean and pressed. Shoes unscuffed, nails neat, clean and unchipped, hair professional and neat. Save the Bubblicious for later (no gum).

Showing up unprepared. Always bring another copy of your resume on high-quality, paper. Always have a pen, notepad/folder to take notes. It makes you look diligent, even if you don't use it or it's just for show. Doesn't matter. It will only help you to stand out. I was most impressed by candidates who immediately took out another copy of their resume and handed it to me.

Being too informal: I once had a candidate back for a 2nd and final in-person interview. It was between he and one other person for a Major Accounts position. Although I was leaning towards him, I was still on the fence. Unfortunately for him, he made the decision easy for me.

He arrives at the reception desk downstairs. As he had been to my office prior, I had the receptionist send him up directly. Next thing I know, he flies into my office, dressed way too casually, tosses his keys on my desk, gum in his mouth and greets me—"hey girl!" Not kidding. Don't do that.

Clean up your social media pages

Before a candidate is hired, many companies informally vet the candidate's personal life, as another data point of his/her lifestyle and character. Most businesses want to ensure that new team members are in basic alignment with that company's core values, whatever they may be.

Google your own name, and you'll probably see social media accounts, images, video, etc connected to your name. Let's say you've applied to be the Director of a Sober Living facility. The hiring manager will of course check references, confirm information supplied on your resume and Job Application.

If they check your FB or IG, and there you are, in all your glory—performing an amazing, death-defying Keg-Stand ... ummm, you'll probably need to continue the job search. Impressive? Yes. Appropriate for employers? Not even close.

Before beginning your search—either change your privacy settings to "friends only" or "private account" OR go through the pictures you've posted with a critical eye and remove any that you think may be questionable. Just use good judgement.

Start building "Good Reputation Equity" first day on the job!

I'll let you in on a secret: *The most advantageous time to build a good professional reputation, is your first year at a new company.* The way you act and perform in the first year, seals your reputation at that company, to a large degree.

Why? Simple. All eyes are always on new-hires. That includes your peers, direct boss, and higher-ups. Don't you naturally want to assess the new guy/gal in your department? I did!

As a new-hire, others are naturally watching you, monitoring your performance, tracking results, noting your work ethic, how-you-conduct yourself, and how well you work with others.

Taking extra care to invest in building a good reputation the first year, puts "markers" in your pocket. Meaning, you're going to have a degree of leniency to tap into, should you need. You'll have earned a level of value—which can translate to consideration for promotions, prime projects, better assignments, opinions that hold more weight, etc. Make sense?

That does not mean you can slack off, after the first year. These are smart practices for your whole career. This is just to ensure that you get started on the right foot.

The 6 Best Career Practices in RULE #19 are universal to any industry. They serve as a good foundation on which to build.

RULE #18
6 best career practices for building "Good Reputation Equity".

Think of your first year, like being in one of those money-grab-tubes they used to have on game shows. You know, stand in a tube with money up to your knees—they turn on the wind machine, and you have 1-minute to grab as much cash as you can. Grab as many "points" as you can your first year. It will serve you well.

Here are my 6 Best-Practices for building Good Reputation Equity your 1st year. That being said—they are important practices for success, in general. In other words, don't let your foot off the gas after year 1—they're always important.

6 Best-Practices:

1. FILO: First In Last Out
2. Always beat Deadlines
3. Be shrewd with company money
4. Don't Complain. Present the challenge, with 2 proposed solutions

5. Under-promise and over-deliver. Make yourself look good!
6. Watch your alcohol: 2-drink maximum. Seriously.

1. Always be FILO: First In Last Out.

Make a commitment, to be the first one in the office and the last one out, at night. Get noticed immediately, by your boss *and* senior level managers for all the right reasons. Why? Because higher-ups are usually in the office early, and last to leave.

Ergo—very quickly, they will notice little ole you, putting in the time, burning the midnight oil. First impressions last forever. This is *such an easy way to rack up brownie points, it'd be foolish not to take advantage of it.*

Chances are, your bosses, boss . . . .will give her a pat on the back, for making a "good hire", which in turn, puts you in her good graces. That is a good thing. You are building equity. Sounds like a pretty easy way to earn extra points, and it is.

Ordinary people do the bare minimum. Equity Builders, do extra:

— Ordinary people show-up exactly at starting time.
— Equity-builders arrive a little early, to get settled and organized for the day.
— Ordinary people are like Fred Flintstone at quitting time. Yabba-dabba-do as soon as the whistle blows.

— *Equity-builders* stay later. Whether it is to finish a project, answer emails or clear their plate of ancillary items that would otherwise cut into the next day's production.

2. Always beat a deadline: Get all work-product in, prior to the assigned deadline.

For me, a deadline of Friday 5pm, means 5pm is the absolute latest. Although I'd never ding someone for a 5pm delivery, I couldn't help but note that they were coming in right under the wire. My favorites, *(shhh!)* were the team members who consistently beat my requested deadline.

I naturally attributed to them, stronger organizational skills, better time management, and discerned they probably put in extra time to get it done. Check, check, and CHECK!

Now, you're building equity. In the future, chances are you'll have an emergency, or a need to request an extension. No problem. You have a solid history of being responsible and accountable. You've earned equity!

3. Be shrewd with company money

If the company gives you an expense account for client meetings, entertainment, pays for travel expenses associated with the job, etc., make it a point to *always* come in *under* the allowance. Why? Because the vast majority of your peers will expense right up to the limit. Consistently coming in under or even well-under, will make you stand out. You'll have "exercises good judgement, can be trusted" equity next to your name.

If you are unsure if an expense is "ok"—make it a point to ask. The mere fact that you ask, scores brownie points.

Side Note: As a Regional VP, I had a $400 gas allowance, which was very generous at the time. Meaning, it was highly unlikely for a VP to use that much in a month. I always logged mileage honestly, expensing maybe $200. While visiting my boss at Corporate, he made it a point to say, "You're the only one who doesn't use the full gas allowance." I thought it was a weird thing to note, given the level of our discussions. He later said, "that's when I knew I could trust you." Point is, he saw it as a mark of honesty, not taking advantage of the company, and acting responsibly.

4. Don't complain. Present the challenge, with 2 proposed solutions

Every company, whether small, large or mega-huge, has its issues and problems. It could be a crappy product, flawed system, annoying colleagues, out-of-touch executives, or a myriad of other issues. I have never, *ever* worked for a perfect company. Because they don't exist.

Those who get ahead, are the ones who understand this, *and seek to resolve*, not whine.

When you come up against challenges and frustration (and you will), here is what NOT to do:

— **Do not complain, whine and commiserate about it with peers.** If you commonly do this, it *will* get back to your boss, and he/she will not like it. Complainers are seen as a cancer in the group, because they are. Their toxicity contaminates the rest of the group, creating a destructive environment.

> **Side Note:** I terminated a high-producing sales rep for this. Despite her value as a high-producer, her negativity was unraveling the entire group. I gave her one fair warning, then terminated her when it happened again. That's how important, the proper handling of issues and challenges is.

— **Do not complain to your boss.** There is a way to address challenges and seek guidance, and a way not to. Constantly going into your boss' office and just "dumping" a problem on his/her desk, with an exasperated tone, shows a lack of maturity, and inability to devise solutions. People who take this route, will never rise up the ladder. Leaders have to problem-solve, and brainstorm solutions.

Present challenges and frustrations to your boss like this:

— Calmly outline the challenge at hand.
— Outline how it is affecting you/company/client. Keep emotion out.
— *Present 2 potential solutions to the challenge.*
— End by asking "What are your thoughts?"

Taking the above approach, will immediately separate you from the rest of your peers. It demonstrates a high level of professionalism and challenge-resolution skills, which are good leadership traits.

This has management material written all over it *(I loved "Office Space"). Your boss will love you for a couple reasons:*

First, the approach reflects a level of maturity and business savvy. Now you've positioned yourself as solutions-based, not problems-based.

Second, you've done the work *for* her! Or at least some of it. Instead of dumping a problem to solve at her feet, like a 3-year old saying "fix my toy!" . . . . you've done the work, *taking the task off of her plate.* At the very least, you have provided a platform for discussion. Either way—good equity!

5. Under-promise and over-deliver. Make yourself look good!

This is important. Don't be the big-talker who can't deliver. While you don't necessarily want to undersell yourself, be mindful of over-selling. Take it back a notch or two, from what you know you can deliver. That way, you've set expectations slightly lower (Under-promise), yet will deliver more than what you promised (over deliver).

For example, if you promise to have deliverables to a client by Friday, but instead deliver on Thursday, you've under-promised and over-delivered. You're looking good.

6. It *seemed* like a good idea at the time . . . watch your alcohol: 2-drink maximum

If I had a penny for every CEM (Career Ending Move), that was fueled by too much alcohol at a company event, I'd buy an island. Sometimes they're really funny to watch . . . well, ok . . . they're almost *always really* funny to watch when it's not you!

Here's the thing. We all want to cut loose and have fun. Companies know the value that reward trips, holiday parties, celebratory dinners, sales-kick-off's and the like, have on overall morale and good feelings toward the organization. They're important. That's why businesses will shell out tens, sometimes hundreds of thousands of dollars to do it.

More often than not, alcohol is a part of this. It sort of fuels the fun, right? Sure. *It can also obliterate everything you've worked to achieve, in one night, if you aren't careful.* You can go from promotable—to sidelined in an instant, or worse yet . . . fired. I've seen it happen.

Even if you don't completely act a fool, do you really want bosses and executives to see you slurring words and wobbling around in your holiday dress and 4" heels? No. At the very least, they'll note poor judgement. Not good.

For this reason, I always always, advised my teams of a *2-drink maximum* at any company or work-sponsored event, conference or networking event. I cared for them and didn't want to see anyone lose a job, or the respect of others, due to sloppy decisions.

My pitch before any event was this: "You can do what you want, but I'd advise a 2-drink maximum . . . you don't want to be the chick dancing on the dinner table with a lampshade on her head, right? . . ." There was a very good reason I did this, as you'll see from this next true story . . .

Keepin' It Real . . . a career-ending move for the records

Truth—I am *so grateful* that I got to witness this just a few years into my career. No one's ever accused me of being a stick-in-the-mud, so watching what too many cocktails at a company event could do, caused me to forever slow my roll! It probably saved me. This story, is the sole "why" behind my 2-drink maximum philosophy.

I was a sales executive for a large Telecomm company. Every year, as most companies do, they hosted a big Sales-Kick-Off at a destination resort, whereby sales teams from every office across the US flew in to attend the 3-day event.

This particular year, it was at the Broadmoor in Colorado Springs, a very fancy resort with gorgeous scenic mountain views, valets, bell-hops, the whole shebang.

The itinerary called for everyone to arrive Friday afternoon, check in, relax—then get ready for the big Welcome Party that night. Present, would be all 300 sales execs, managers, directors, VP's and the entire C-level Executive team, including the CEO who flew in from NYC.

As was the trend, no expense was spared. There were *multiple* full-service bars throughout, cocktail servers passing around endless supplies of "specialty shots," food up to the ceiling, an amazing DJ spinning the tunes, lots of dancing, and basically... teetering on the edge of debauchery. I think this is why I got into sales. Salespeople always know how to have a good time.

Oh, and I might add that the actual "Kick-Off" conference, started at 7:30am the next morning. So there's that.

Telecomm was known for being one of the most competitive, hard-core industries to be in, especially for sales. The average salesperson lasted 3 months. That's 12-weeks. It was so brutal, so demanding, very few could take the stress and pressure—and either left or were fired. Those who lasted (I lasted 10 years), had hard-charging, tough, competitive, Type-A personalities. It was the work-hard-play-hard mentality, on steroids.

A few hours into it, we're all having fun, dancing, drinking, socializing—when for whatever reason, the tone of a woman's voice caught my attention. You know those times, when something just sounds *different*—so you turn to look.

I see our CEO, who was probably in his early 70's, very conservative, dressed in a navy suit and tie, white hair with a hard-part, sprayed down like a helmet. Next to him, his equally conservative wife complete with oversized blazer, skirt 3" below the knee, turtleneck, pearls and brown helmet hair—clutching a glass of wine, looking stunned—and for good reason.

A female sales exec from another office, who clearly had *way* too much to drink, *had started shouting lewd obscenities at his (the CEO's) wife.* In the blink of an eye, she then stepped 6" from the CEO's face and shoved him, shouted more obscenities at the wife—then *shoved her.*

It happened so fast, and I think we were all trying to digest what was unfolding in front of us. I mean, that sort of behavior is so unheard of—you question your interpretation of the scene. Pretty quickly, a rush of guys ran over, and pulled the sales woman away. I don't really remember the rest of the details, except everything ended shortly thereafter everyone buzzing like crazy about what happened.

The next morning, everyone is still buzzing about it. The sales exec was fired (duh) first thing the next morning and booked on the next flight home. I had heard, that as she was waiting to be taken to the airport... She was at the BAR *having a cocktail.*

That's an extreme story, but it is also a true story. Life is all about choices. Many times we learn from our own mistakes, and sometimes, if we're observant and mindful—we have the privilege of learning from the mistakes of *others.*

A positive reputation on the job is yours to win or lose. Choose to win it.

BADASS
LIFE STRATEGIES

Confidence is Silent. Insecurities are Loud.

> ## RULE #19
> Identify your key strengths, then leverage them. Don't waste time trying to be Britney.

You can do anything you put your mind to . . . I'll take "Urban Myths for $200, Alex."

I know it's really trendy to tell people and kids, "You can do anything you put your mind to," and truthfully, I do understand the well-intentioned *why* behind it.

Archaic cultural paradigms that said, "you can't do that because you're a girl," or "you can't do that because you didn't go to college/the right college/don't have proper training/don't fit the mold," etc., were and *are* unfairly limiting to those who do not fit into subjective, pre-defined molds.

We *do* want to shatter and break free of self-imposed and society-imposed limitations, that do nothing other than put a muzzle on our own potential and growth. That is a very, very good thing.

However, the problem I see is this: In an effort to break free of the old, we have pushed the Pendulum from a metaphoric 3:00, all the way to 9:00. From one extreme to another extreme. We see this playing out, in an inherent *lack of reason* in terms of goal setting, which many times serves to set ourselves and kids up for disappointment and failure.

Why? Because we need to *first* understand *where our natural strengths and talents lie,* **then** build big dreams around those talents. From there, "you can do anything if you work hard, and want it enough," is more than possible!

Swim with the tide, not against it

When we work *with* our strengths, we are swimming *with* the tide, not against it. That is when we experience the greatest level of success and happiness. The realization of our dreams feels almost effortless.

If we build dreams around talents or skills that candidly—we flat out do not have, we are choosing to work harder, not smarter. We swim against the tide, working harder with less traction, living a life less than we were meant to live.

If god gave you a particular strength or talent—it's because you are supposed to do something with it!

It's Britney, B*tch. No matter how badly I want to be her—it's not gonna happen.

I love Britney. When her video comes on, I jump up, swing my head, attempt Hip-Hop without twisting an ankle, and try breathlessly to sing along while doing a backbend. Listen, I'm telling you—the dogs *like it*!

But here's the sad truth: No matter how hard I work, or how badly I want it, I am not going to be Britney, or even a famous singer in my own right. Why? *Because I cannot sing*. I know that, and fully acknowledge it. I am awful. I can't event stand to listen to myself and turn up the radio. I mean, it's really bad.

Had I ignored this fact, and instead insisted on pursuing a career in music because "it's my dream", and *Mom said* I could do anything I wanted . . . Uhhhh, it would have been a very long, painful, fruitless road for me.

And she bangs, she bangs . . .

Remember watching American Idol? How many times did you absolutely cringe at some of the contestants who clearly could not sing a note, but seemed to be living in an alternate universe, insisting they were going to be a huge star and wouldn't stop until they got there. Didn't we all think "How can you be that oblivious??"

I can almost guarantee, they were the kids who were told they could achieve anything, if they wanted it badly enough and worked hard.

I know this may sound harsh to some, as the truth can sometimes be. I believe strongly, in removing self-imposed limitations and believing in yourself. I built a career out of it. That being said, *let's work smarter, not harder.* Let's seek to apply *balance and realism*, by first defining our natural strengths and talents, **then** building and aligning big dreams with those talents.

Having ambition without focus, is like plunking a mouse down into a huge field and saying, "Find the most efficient path to the finish line." It'll take the mouse an inordinate amount of time and frustration to find the path, if ever.

The *ABC Bucket's* Approach

The *ABC Bucket's* approach, was a highly effective, popular method I devised when leading sales organizations. The sole purpose, was to help each team member clearly define their own Key Strengths and Key Challenges, then help them flesh out goals and dreams, that aligned with those Strengths. It was popular for 3 reasons:

1. Its simplicity.
2. Its effectiveness in creating clarity and focus on a person's Strengths.
3. Its effectiveness in leveraging Strengths, to reach high-goals.

Here's How it Works:

1. Take out a piece of paper.
2. At the top, in 3 columns write A, B, C, across the page.
3. Next, jot down your own Strengths and Non-Strengths under each column—according to the definitions below.

Side Note: Strengths aren't what you would *like* to be good at, they are areas that you *know* you're good at . . .

Bucket A = *The Strengths in Bucket A are your Jam! These are your "I was born this way, baby!" strengths.* When exercising these skills and aptitudes, you feel completely in your element—like a fish swimming with the flow of fast-rushing water. You barely have to paddle to move along quickly! It feels good, and you are good at it.

Bucket B = *The Strengths in Bucket B don't feel as natural as A's, but with a little work and effort, you master them well-enough to include them in your core-strengths.* I usually divided this bucket into B and B+, which would be included in core-strengths, while a B- was considered a Non-Strength.

Bucket C = *This is Square-Peg-in-a-Round-Hole Bucket,* named because it would be easier to get the square peg through the hole, than to be even remotely good in these areas. *These are your Non-Strengths.* I jokingly referred to it as the "Don't even think about it," bucket.

I promise, you intuitively know what they are. They feel flat-out awkward, difficult and frustrating. You secretly suspect, when god was handing out these particular skills—you were taking a nap. As such, you probably really dislike having to do them.

Next Step: A 2nd Set of Eyes . . .

Look at your ABC's. Do your categorizations ring true? *Now, ask someone you trust to review your list and give their honest, thoughtful input.* I've found that many times, other people see important talents that we hadn't even considered.

Here's a big one: . . . If something comes to us really easily, *we are more likely to dismiss it as an actual Strength.* We usually tell ourselves *"That's not a big deal—everyone can do that."* Chances are, that's not true!

We *think* everyone can do it, because it is *easy for us*! That's why it's important to have someone close, whose opinion you value, act as a 2nd set of eyes. It's so helpful in defining each and every Strength!

Putting it to Use: Focus on A's and B's. Sideline the C's.

Focus on creating, envisioning and following a path, that capitalizes and leverages your Key Strengths. These are your

A and B Buckets. Let A's serve as the primary guidance, with B's playing a supportive role. This is how you focus and leverage. C's are going to get sidelined.

Resist the temptation to "tackle and master" C's. They are a red-herring. Meaning, they only serve to distract and derail. These are areas you are going to outsource to others. Whether that means hiring people who specialize in your 'C's, or forming a partnership with someone who's A's and B's, are your C's.

Example:

I have a friend who is a very talented artist, but she's also a skilled people person. People are drawn to her, and she effortlessly creates business opportunities that have worked to positively expand her business.

She cringes at the thought of negotiating contracts, fee agreements or vetting software programs for their infrastructure.

Her *(simplified)* ABC Buckets look like this:

A = Creative, talented artist
B = People skills and networking
C = Business mechanics, infrastructure, contract and business negotiations

Based on the above, it is *smartest* for her to focus all her energy, on showcasing her artistry, and creating opportunities through networking, while outsourcing "C". Which is what she has done.

Instead of banging her head against the wall, trying to master her "C's", she brought on a Partner who *specializes* in those areas (Her C's, are his A's). Thus, freeing herself to really capitalize on what she does best.

The result, is that she has created a much bigger, more successful business, than had she insisted on doing everything herself.

Closing notes . . .

I once watched an interview with Bill Gates, talking about the success of Microsoft. The interviewer was effusive in her praise of his brilliance, skill and foresight in building a world-class organization. Instead of basking in the praise, he was quick to step aside, and shine the light on his Microsoft team.

Paraphrasing, he said that great organizations are never built solely by one person in a vacuum. Rather, they are built on the backs of an entire team, each bringing their own set of unique and differing skills, talents and contributions to the table. He may have had the idea—but without the team, it is just that. An idea.

I never forgot this. In my professional life, I noted that the most successful, most admired, confident and respected people, were those who fully understood their Strengths, but more importantly—understood and embraced their weaknesses. They capitalized on their own Strengths, recruited key talent to fill in where they lacked, and in the end—created iron strong organizations.

By clearly understanding and defining our natural strengths, we lead much happier, more fulfilling lives. No one likes to feel unsuccessful. We've all felt the sting of failure, and it isn't fun. Capitalize, focus on and leverage your Key Strengths. Let go of the C's.

Trying to build a dream or goal, around your C's, no matter how badly you really, really want to be Britney, is a recipe for disappointment and frustration. It's also a bass-ackwards approach.

Define your Strengths FIRST, then build your amazing goals and dreams around them!

RULE #20

Slow your roll—hold your anger for 24-hours.

Badass women know the power of controlling their emotions, especially anger. The second you lose your cookies and start yelling, is the same second you lose power and respect. The second you fire off a snarky, knee-jerk reaction email, is the same second your stock drops.

Badass women know that the scariest thing in the world, is a silent, smiling woman. Right? Aside from the fact that it will scare the crap out of most anyone, initial silence and a steady gaze into the eyes of the other person, can be an extremely powerful, effective weapon.

During a negotiation, the other side will fill in what you are thinking—to their detriment. Many times they'll start back-peddling and making concessions without you having to utter a word. Sometimes I use it on my husband, truth be told.

Anger is a loss of control

Some of the biggest personal and professional mistakes are made in the heat of anger. Anger is a form of loss of control.

That's why we say and do things we later regret. Today, there is the added element of the digital world, which means an angry email or online outburst not only travels at lightning speed, but it's right there in black and white for all to see ... forever.

At work, angry, knee-jerk reactions will erode your promotability. You'll be seen as a loose cannon, ineffective in the face of adversity, with poor conflict resolution skills, and basically look like an ass. You cannot promote someone who is incapable of expressing anger in a controlled, effective manner. They'll self-combust, reflecting poorly on the company.

In personal life, angry outbursts can permanently damage relationships, marriages and hurt the people you love. That isn't good for anyone.

Chill out for 24-hours

Next time you find yourself pounding out an angry email to a friend or co-worker, or constructing a snarky social media rant, before hitting "Send," WAIT 24-hours. I promise, you will either delete the email and be really happy that you did, OR you will rewrite your points in a much more professional, diplomatic way. Either way, you'll be thankful that you waited.

Next time someone hits your hot-button, and you feel that all too familiar knee-jerk reaction welling up inside ... Walk away. Say "I need to walk away from this right now.

Let's revisit it tomorrow." WAIT 24-hours, or at least until you've had time to calm down.

I get that work-related issues generally can't wait 24-hours for one to calm down. I'm usually ready to revisit the conversation pretty quickly, if I step away and work on another project for an hour or so.

In other words, slow your roll and wait a day before responding either in person or in an email. If you need to vent, get it all out of your system in an email *without sending*. Make sure the "To" field is blank, so it's not accidentally sent. That would be awkward.

If you wait a day, 9 times out of 10 you will not send the email as it was originally written. Your message will soften and be far more productive in resolving the situation. It's sort of like *drunk-texting*... you really don't want to wake up the next morning, mortified at what you sent. You would never have sent that, sober!! Same idea.

RULE #21

Understand the power of your Personal Image. Let it communicate who you are and where you want to go, *at-a-glance*.

Personal image, is the *perception* that other people have about who you are. It affects your success in virtually every area of life – career, social, and even personal relationships. This is because no matter who you are, the image others have of you, plays an important role in your success.

The way the world sees you, determines the opportunities that come, *or do not* come your way. It is an element in whether your path is *easier* or *harder*. Make it *easier* by playing the game strategically.

Badass women understand this concept. The way she dresses, speaks, holds herself, relates to others and reacts to situations, are key elements she uses to her advantage in shaping her own powerful personal image.

To be clear, this does *not* mean pretending to be someone you are not—badass women aren't fakey posers. Rather, it's *highlighting* on the outside, *who you are on the inside* in order to invite success your way.

Example:

You've just graduated from college with a degree in Architecture. Super smart, graduating at the very top of your class, you can't wait to take the world by storm with your ambition, drive and creative talent. The world is yours for the taking.

The goal is to land a position with a top firm. These firms are very conservative in nature. On paper, you've got what it takes but the field is competitive. Landing an interview is hard.

But you are a hustler—a mover and a shaker! In addition to sending out resumes, you work tirelessly, networking like crazy with industry groups and industry influencers—hoping someone will help you to land an interview.

Knowing the industry is conservative—if you show up to networking events (or a job interview) with a purple mohawk and nose-ring, chomping on bubble gum and dropping F-bombs, do you think anyone is going to help you land an interview?

The answer is NO. You could be the most talented, creative architect ever to walk the earth—but no one will know. You have created a more difficult path for yourself.

Instead—Learn to play the game

Understand the conservative nature of the industry and play the game, if you want "in". Highlight on the outside, the smarts, ambition, drive and creative talent that you have on the inside. Seek to inspire immediate confidence at-a-glance. In other words, dress to look the part, for the job you want.

Save the mohawk, nose ring and f-bombs for later. Spit your gum out. Create your image in ways that facilitate your goals and make your path easier not harder.

Consider these 2 scenarios. Same person—different image. Who wins?

Scenario A

I have been hired to speak to a large professional group, on the Keys to Success. The audience is filled with 2,500 professionals eagerly awaiting my pearls of wisdom. The lights dim, the announcer comes on stage to introduce me, the illustrious speaker who shall now show them the way to the promised land of professional success. They can't wait.

He finishes my impressive introduction, they clap eagerly—and out I come, in all my glory. For the event, feast your eyes on me in my *favorite* black Lulu Lemon stretch pants, my beach flip-flops because they're comfy and I know I'll be standing for a while.... And of course my *infamous* USD college sweatshirt, circa 1994. So worn, it feels like cashmere, and maybe a spaghetti sauce stain or two that I couldn't get out. Oh well, no one will notice.

Instead of confidently working the stage back and forth, I sit Indian-style in a chair, low-energy, shoulders hunched, hands folded in my lap, mumbling my words into a microphone. Have I inspired confidence in the audience? No. They can't stand me and can't believe they came to the event.

It doesn't matter how brilliant my presentation is, nor how awe-inspiring my Success Tips are—I have already lost the game, based solely on the image I chose to present. I needlessly sabotaged myself. No Bueno.

Scenario B

Assume the same scenario as above, with the same speech-presentation content. Only this time, I bound onto the stage with bright energy, smiling confidently and extending my hand warmly to thank the announcer. Dressed sharply in professional wide-legged navy trousers, an open, fitted navy jacket and silk, fuchsia printed blouse with neck-bow (ok, I like clothes)... I take the microphone and begin working the stage back and forth as I graciously and clearly thank the audience for coming.

Now I've got everyone's attention! Do you think they're excited and ready to listen? Of course they are!

Same "me," same speech-presentation. The only difference is the image *I chose* to convey.

I'm not pretending to be anyone I am not—*I'm just being smart about my external image.* If I was going to teach Yoga—I'd wear the Lulu outfit. That would inspire confidence in Yogi's. Plus, a suit would be really hot and awkward in a heated yoga class.

RULE #22
Know your *End-Game*. It will naturally drive your decisions and your actions.

Your *End-Game* is the *result* you want, from any given situation. It acts as both destination and compass, guiding decisions and actions that are in alignment with that End-Game. It provides focus and direction, like a rudder.

> *For example*, if getting into law school is your End-Game, that will naturally dictate what courses you decide to take in college, it'll push you to study harder or forgo a few parties here and there in pursuit of good grades, you may seek summer jobs at local firms, etc.

If your end-game is a promotion into management, you will be extra mindful to make decisions in both words and actions, that are in alignment with that position.

End-games are both large and small, short-term and long-term. They are in our professional lives as well as our personal lives. End-games guide your actions, but even more importantly—they work to eliminate battles that you may otherwise engage in.

Picking your battles

An equally important benefit of first defining your end-game, is that it forces you in a way, to pick your battles. It's an unhealthy, unproductive life distraction to fight every battle that gets your goat. You'll spend your life expending needless energy fighting, instead of building.

When you are clear on what does and what does not lead you towards your goal, it is much easier to let the small things go.

Personal-life example:

I think a lot of families can identify with this little gem. It's Thanksgiving Day. The entire family is over, enjoying food, family, football and cocktails—when *someone* decides... *it's time to talk politics.* Because what could possibly be more relaxing? You can practically see the train derail in slow-mo.

At this point, you have 2 choices:

1. Get sucked into it, as Thanksgiving is ruined with escalating tensions.
2. Ignore, de-escalate, let it go and enjoy the day.

If your *end-game* is to enjoy family, feel thankful and create warm family memories—you'll choose #2. Isn't that more important?

If you hadn't thought about your "goal" for the day, it would be extremely easy to get sucked into the vortex, ending up angry and upset over opinions that in the grand scheme, aren't changing anything. The only real result, is a ruined dinner.

I personally, always choose #2 in social settings. When topics or opinions that I disagree with are voiced in these settings, I immediately think of 2 things:

1. My end-game is to enjoy a nice evening.
2. Nothing productive will come from counter-arguing, except ruining the evening.

My 'go-to' tactics, are:

1. Ignore the comments.
2. Change the subject.
3. Excuse myself to the restroom, or anything that I feel will break the negative energy.

Professional-life example:

Professionally, it's extra important to define your end-game. Knowing what you want (your goal), will guide the way you conduct yourself, respond to criticism, obstacles, and challenging people or situations. It plays a key role in determining how far you go. It defines your promotability, and even whether or not you keep your job.

I am thinking of one particular woman I knew. She was smart, understood the industry better than anyone, and was technically, very good at her job. She had the opportunity and core-abilities to rise to the top. Unfortunately, she was not only deemed unpromotable, she couldn't keep a job for longer than a couple years.

Why? If you asked her "What's your end-game? What it is your ultimate goal?".... she probably wouldn't know.

This woman went about each day, *reacting* to challenges, people, clients and situations blindly, instead of *strategically. Tick her off in a meeting?* You were sure to get a seething email, clearly written in anger and fired-off without a cooling down period. Oh—and a cc to the CEO and CFO for good measure.

Disagree or challenge her? Angry outburst + storming out of the office. *Challenging client?* Condescending demeanor, which usually meant the client escalated the issue to a senior manager (lucky me).

Conversely, **if she had a defined *end-game*,** perhaps a promotion to Sr. Director or Division Head, for example, that defined end-game would have worked to guide her behavior in ways *aligned with her goals.*

Instead of firing off seething emails, the thought may have been:

> *"I'm not going to respond right now. I'm angry, and I don't want to look like a loose cannon. I'll cool down, then construct a well-laid out counter-argument, reflective of a Sr. Director . . . which is my goal."*

This is an extreme example, given more to illustrate a point. Most people aren't such hot-heads.

That being said, you get the point: Defining your endgame, will help you to act, react and respond in ways that work to push you *towards* your goal, not away. That's what we all want for ourselves!

Git it, Girl! Final Thoughts . . .

My hope is that as human-beings, we arrive at a point in our evolution whereby a woman who is unapologetically self-confident, uncompromising in her standards, independent and all of that good stuff, *isn't such an anomaly that she is given a special label.* In this case—a Badass.

It isn't always easy to implement every one of the 22 Rules. At least at first. Some people in your life will push back when you begin to stand your ground. Some "friends" may fall to the wayside. Strength, confidence and self-worth are intimidating to some. Let it work itself out. Some of those friends will adjust, others will just go away. Either way, *let the tree prune itself.*

My suggestion is to work on the 22 Rules in batches. Find 3 or 4 Rules that seem easiest for you and start there. Once you've integrated them into your life, identify 2 others that feel more challenging. Keep adding by 2 or 3, as you feel ready.

That's how you get there!

Remember, you were born with a Badass inside you! *We all were.* She is smiling in anticipation, eagerly rubbing her hands together—ready for you unleash her.

A Badass is:

A way of thinking, behaving and moving through the world with unapologetic self-confidence, uncompromising self-worth, assertiveness, compassion, independence, comfort in her own skin and grace under fire.

Let's get after it!

22 BADASS RULES CHECKLIST

Badass STANDARDS: GUYS, DATING and RELATIONSHIPS

#1 Teach men how to treat you: Set your standards and stick to them.

#2 No one puts Baby in a corner! You aren't anyone's Plan B.

#3 Never chase a guy. Ever. If he's interested, he'll come to you.

#4 When a guy tells you by his actions, who he is—believe him. The first time.

#5 (6) Universal Red Flags that translate to: GAME OVER.

#6 Keep the values that make you feel strong—release all the others.

#7 Expect CHIVALRY: It does matter... and NO it is not sexist.

#8 WAIT until he asks for Exclusivity.

#9 Ending relationships, pull-off the band-aid fast and hard. It's less painful.

#10 Watch how a man talks about and treats his mom. It'll tell you how he feels about women, and it's indicative of how he will treat you.

Badass LIFE FUNDAMENTALS

#11 Your life is 10% what happens to you, 90% how you handle it.
#12 The fine art of not giving a f*ck.
#13 Life's BIGGEST mistakes are made when we ignore our intuition.
#14 Live the life that makes YOU happy.
#15 The 5 people you spend the most time with, either add to detract from your life course. Choose mindfully and wisely.
#16 Understand that you always have the power of choice. Always.

One Badass CAREER

#17 80% of getting the job, is just not being an idiot.
#18 (6) best career practices for building "Good Reputation Equity".

Badass LIFE STRATEGIES

#19 Identify your key strengths, then leverage them. Don't waste time trying to be Britney.
#20 Slow your roll—hold your anger for 24-hours.
#21 Understand the power of your Personal Image. Let it communicate who you are and where you want to go, at-a-glance.
#22 Know your END-GAME. It will naturally drive decisions and actions towards your goal.

SHELLI PELLY is an award-winning, former corporate leader, known for her unique ability to coach others beyond their own self-imposed limitations.

Known for her inspiring candor, laser-insight, humor and optimism, Shelli combines straight-forward talk with clearly defined goals, coaching women of all ages towards becoming an authentically strong, confident and more empowered version of themselves.

Made in the USA
Middletown, DE
04 December 2018